Larry Ukali
Johnson-Redd

History To
Destiny
Through
Afrocentric
Poetry

History to Destiny, Through Afrocentric Poetry
Copyright © 2025 by Larry Ukali Johnson-Redd

ISBN: 979-8894791982 (sc)
ISBN: 979-8894791999 (e)

The Reading Glass Books
(888) 420-3050
www.readingglassbooks.com
fulfillment@readingglassbooks.com

Acknowledgements

First of all, I want to dedicate this book to GOD and all of GOD'S goodness.

Secondly, I also want to dedicate this book to my sister Sharon and her husband James Brown, Jr. Sharon typed the final draft and James and her laid it down in the CD format.

Thirdly I would like to dedicate this book of Afro-Centric Poetry to my Mom, Mrs. Berdine Redd and the loving memory of my Dad, the Late Mr. Henry Redd Sr. I would also like to dedicate this book to my Dad who made me, the Late Mr. Elijah Johnson.

Fourthly, I would like to dedicate this book to all my Brothers and Sisters in my family and all my Brothers and Sisters around the world that would include my Cousins, Aunts other Relatives and In- Laws.

Fifthly, I would like to dedicate this book to all victims of slavery, police and prison guard brutality as well as all of those people who want struggle for freedom all over the world from Southern Sudan to West Papua, New Guinea to the American West Coast, to the West Indies to East, North, South and West Africans and to Africans and African-Americans between all of those points.

I want to dedicate this book to all freedom fighters that want the world to be free including Africans and African-Americans throughout Canada, Europe and the Middle East. In fact this book is dedicated to the Palestinians struggling to free occupied Palestine. And to those who support freedom from occupation for all people all over the world.

And last, I dedicate this book to Dwayne Tomell Mayberry, my homie who was 1 of about 10 co-founders of the 1986-90 San Francisco Black United Front, and passed away in late July 2003 and another brother I grew up with Everett Adams who passed away in August or September 2003.

Editorial Note

The poems herein represent three decades, beginning in the late 1960's to the year 2003.

Date Reviewed: January 27, 2005

HISTORY TO DESTINY: Through Afrocentric Poetry by Mr. Larry Ukali Johnson-Redd Amen-Ra Theological Seminary Press, 2003 original not this e publication 303 Pages, Paperback, $20.00 paperback-($.99 cents as a Kindle e-book)
ISBN: 096742268X
Genre: Poetry

RAW Rating: 4
From A Black Man's Perspective

HISTORY TO DESTINY is an abundant collection of poetry which spans three decades of life experiences and perspectives of Mr. Larry Ukali Johnson-Redd. It covers a plethora of topics such as racial injustice, police brutality and economic displacement. It carries a common theme of Black unity, social awareness and self-love.

I was initially reluctant to read the collection, because it is as thick as any novel. But, as I began to read the poems assembled, I respected the author's views on the various subjects covered. The words he utilized were simple and the subject matter of each poem was always clear. Mr. Johnson-Redd's passion comes across in his poetry, but coupled with the density of the collection, it became overwhelming. After completing the series of poems, I sought a lighter subject to relieve the strain. That is not to take away from the value of HISTORY TO DESTINY, just that one must be prepared to enjoy what it has to offer.

Reviewed by Aiesha Flowers of The RAWSISTAZ™ Reviewers
website:rawsistaz.com

My reading of Mr. Larry Ukali Johnson-Redd's, "History to Destin Through Afrocentric Poetry", was full of poems that radiated with the spirit, the voices and the cry of the elders and our ancestors.

To me, this poetry expresses the great need for the Africans in America to unite with each other and unite with Africans in the Diaspora as well as with Africans all over the world as a conscious priority These sleve comments written by the late Nashid Hakim Ahmad born December 4, 1939 sunrise to June 26, 2011 sunset Rest in Peace my brother

The three decade-plus of poetry presented in this book by brother Larry Ukali Johnson-Redd speaks to the African mind, and challenge readers to consider a protracted dedication to love and human development.

Itibari M. Zulu, Th.D.
Vice President, The African Diaspora Foundation; Provisional Director, King-Luthuli Transformation Centre Peace Library and Distance Learning Centre. Johannesburg, South Africa.

Amen-Ra Theological Seminary Press 10920 Wilshire Boulevard, Suite 150-9132 Los Angeles, California 90024-6502

THREE NEW POEMS WRITTEN IN 2011

Release A Black Dove Of Peace
Written by Larry Ukali Johnson-Redd

To my young brothers
And the O G's too
There is too much conflict
We are Split

Obama is in the white house
We're facing unemployment
And desperation
With benign neglect

We're dieing
In the street
We are killing our
Own heart beat

Throwing out a threat
Unable to protect
Anytime there is death
Common sense brings regret

We must return
To peace in the hood
All these deaths are
No damn good

And the bloodshed
From desperation and children underfed
Many homeless and
Too many dead

When our self love
And our young are dead
We got to stop this craziness
Brother hear what I said

We have a choice
Bring back one love
In our Ghetto or community
One love for you and me

Unless we want
Just what we got
This killing madness
We must stop

Bring us back
To one love
We must release
A black Dove of peace

Tough times financially
For everyone
No telling
what's to come

There is a need
To do more than bleed
Children are wisdom hungry
We must feed

And Sarah Palin and
Tea Party-Republicans
Say let them cookies or cake
They are phony and fake

They are cutting off
Unemployment
More benign neglect
From the government

We have to
Come together
To survive now
To forever

We have to love
Each other better
It is up to us
No other, my sister and brother

And build
An economy
To employ
You and me

We cannot build
In a war with each other
Please think about this
My sister and brother

And stop the blood
We see a run
Cause we all want

To see a better day come

One Percent Greed

By Larry Ukali Johnson-Redd
Author of American Challenges In The Obama Era,
Long Distance Love and Loving Black Women
(Kindle e-books) email- johnson-redd@att.net

Too many have died
For a lack of Healthcare
Too many died
And their relatives cried

And the tea party
They are fried
One day they will say
The tea party died

While they are
Robo signing foreclosures
Un-housing those who can't feed
And those who are in need

Mortgage House, bank
and corporate greed
While the American
Dream is made to bleed

Domination of 1% money
And it's greedy creed
Amid the suffering
of those in need

So how can we say?
We freed
Can you see?
A homeless seed

And the 1% rich gets richer
And the Poverty is thicker
So stress kills the poor
And the profits are bigger

The rich get richer
The poor get no more
Banks and corporations
Corrupt to the core

About the rich 1%
The poor can only vent
We may live on the street
We may live in a tent

Or live 1 step from eviction
Some can't buy a prescription
More corporate greed in the suite
More people in the street

Our jobs exported
Overseas
Here we see
A hiring freeze

And now we see
People's occupation
In opposition to
Corporate exploitation

Bank and corporate greed
And concentrated 1 percent wealth
Is totally bad
For America's health

From bank and corporate dictatorship
Give us People's democracy
From gross economic disparity
Give us economic opportunity

Health care in great jeopardy
So it's hard to live in poverty
The people are exploited the most
Americans occupy Wall Street from coast to coast

Black Romance
One on One
Black Romance
May the joy come

Black Romance
May we advance
Black Romance
Love and happiness

Black Romance
Make it fun
Black Romance"Until the morning sun

Black Romance
For you and me
Black Romance
Sweet as it can be

From her lips
To her pretty nose
Black Romance
For your Black Rose.

Foreword
written by Donald Lacy

I first met Larry Ukali Johnson-Redd in the early 80's at an African Liberation Day celebration Oakland, California, which I emceed. I was struck by his intelligence, warmth and integrity. Our paths have crossed many times since then and no one I have encountered since has been more passionate about the true liberation of our people than he has.

After he returned from his trip from Africa, Ukali gushed openly about his experiences and how the trip to the Motherland had given him a deeper understanding of the plight that many of our brothers and sisters face in America on a daily basis. I have always respected Ukali as a writer and an activist. I interviewed him a number of times on my KPOO FM radio show Wake Up Everybody about a variety of issues that affected the Black community, particularly the brutal and unjust murder of Larry Lumpkin by the San Francisco Police Department.

Over the years I have known Ukali, he has been a consistent advocate for justice and equality for African people everywhere. In his book, History to Destiny Through Afrocentric Poetry, Ukali chronicles his lifetime experiences in America and Africa and pays homage to our ancestors Langston Hughes, Marcus Garvey, Bob Marley, Marvin Gaye and many others.

Ukali speaks of solidarity with African people throughout (Africa) and the Diaspora from Lagos to Grenada and all points between. He reflects on our lives, loves, and struggles against racism, oppression and brutality. But most importantly, he has eloquently captured in these pages the righteousness and victory of our struggle as an oppressed people in this the fifth century since enslavement.

In the tradition of a true Griot, Ukali passes on the ancient practice of putting us in touch with each other, our roots, our blackness, and our birthright so we can renew our commitment to ourselves and our people.

We must continue to carry the torch that so many of our forefathers and mothers did before us. Many who laid down their lives so we could continue to thrive and contribute to the world at large. I am sure after reading this book you will discover a man whose love of our people will undoubtedly serve to awaken the sleeping giant in us all.

Introduction to History to Destiny Through Afrocentric Poetry and More Thoughts on The Importance of Africa to Africans in America or African Americans and Africans all over the world

By Larry Ukali Johnson-Redd

The importance of Africa is central to understanding the heart and soul of African-Americans or more properly Africans in America.

African-Americans live in highly technical modern environment and have no trouble mastering the ways of this society when given a fair chance to use the technology and see its benefits. However, Africans in America like our African brothers and sisters in Africa have been overwhelmed with the white beauty standards promoted all over the west. And, too many of us here and even to a lesser extent our homeland brothers and sisters have similar ways of looking at shades of Black in terms of white western beauty standards. As a result of such thinking there are many Africans in America who use skin lighteners to even their tone or even lighten their tone. African-Americans or Africans anywhere else who use skin lighteners should wise up and stop this crazy behavior that supports white supremacy.

Those of us who are victims of white supremacy should not glorify our oppressors by trying to bleach skin to make it closer to white skin. There are also some Africans in Africa and the Caribbean who use skin lighteners

Hopefully, the majority of Africans all over the world from West Papua and New Guinea to Fuji to Africa to the Caribbean/South America region to North America can appreciate all of the shades of Black that we are as African People producing naturally all shades of Black and no one should prefer or favor one shade of black over another. Peter Tosh the late great Jamaican Reggae singer got it right with his song 'If you are a Black Man, You are an African. African People all over the world naturally produce all shades of Black. And of greatest importance to us is the fact that Africa is the homeland of all Africans all over the world.

We have to value our natural African selves as we were made in all of the beautiful shades of Black that we are. We have to appreciate the natural hair, facial shade, color and features. We must love ourselves consciously never favor any shade of Black that appears to be closer to white skin as the only beautiful African skin. All shades of Black are beautiful. As a people we do need to elevate our self-esteem.

However, when I traveled throughout the various regions of Nigeria (1977 to 1981) it was very obvious to me that each region of Nigeria produced Africans, Nigerians of every shade of black. Every region had albinos without pigment or color who married there in their home region more times than not.

Although some of our Nigerian brothers and sisters are influenced by the extensive propaganda of the west these days, so too are we and yet Nigerians, African-Americans and all other Africans need to look inside our African culture more than following the west or anyone else blindly.

When you are in Warri, Sapele or any other costal Nigerian area or city, you may see some Nigerians with white blood in their veins but they are 100% Nigerians in culture and diet not western. Every region of Nigeria produces albinos who are without pigment. Again, they are completely Nigerian in culture and diet. In Nigeria, people marry brothers and sisters from other tribal communities. And, if we sometimes think from our experience in America think some one who is light is closer to white or mixed with white then we really do not understand that who we are as a people comes from within our African soul. And, like our Nigerian brothers and sisters, we African-Americans produce all of the beautiful shades of Black.

We Africans all over the world have been producing all the beautiful shades of Black since the beginning of time and so shall it be in the future.

In the old brainwashed days some among us said if you are—you are all right, if you are brown stay around and if you are black get back.

This was apart of the divide and conquer or divide and rule strategy developed at the dawn of slavery and detailed in the historic Willie Lynch letter. But, let us teach ourselves and future generations that each and every shade of Africa is Black and Beautiful.

African people all over the world come from Africa. All shades of Black are African. All shades of Black are African historically and culturally and our color is our gift from Africa our motherland no matter what shade of Black it is. And, that is the importance of Africa, the source of Blackness that embraces all of us no matter what beautiful shades of Black we may be.

If we can practice a real love and respect for ourselves as a people then maybe our precious young people will value each other realistically instead of fighting and internal wars we see too often in our communities. Black is beautiful and it is so beautiful to be Black. Today Nigeria's unity and indeed the unity of the entire African continent our motherland is divided by divided governments and religious differences regarding religions that are not controlled by Africans. This is a major challenge to Africa and Africans all over the world.

The answer lies in the development of a United States of Africa that could compete with the USA, China, Europe, Russia, and Indonesia. I will discuss this challenge facing Africans, Asians, African Americans, Americans, Caribbean's and Melanesians more completely in my next book American Challenges in the Obama Era Part 2 but suffice it to say if there were to be a United States of the Caribbean and a United States of Africa as well as a United States of Melanesia by any other name, we the Black Skinned people of the world would be far more empowered to take on the world corporate elite and in the case of Melanesia and Melanesians who are related to use by African blood, the Indonesians.

However please read History to Destiny Through Afrocentric Poetry and my other books and join me on face book through my long name to discuss my books and issues raised around empowerment for the divided and powerless Black skinned people in the world and let us discuss these natters so we can join the world as equally empowered with the rest of the people of the world.

The culture War in America prolific and comprehensive; however, it is also stealth like in the sense that it is subliminal and not always out in the open. However, this culture war is totally applied to African Americans no matter how we identify ourselves all over this country. This culture war seeks to steal authentic African-American expressions in many ways such as "right on" and paint them white.

America through its subliminal culture war frowns on anything African such as African lips or thick African lips, African shapes, African speech patterns and African American conscious music including conscious rap, conscious soul/rhythm and Blues, Conscious writing, conscious poetry and other African forms of expression.

Fashion icons have broken ranks by endorsing the beauty of full lips, full African lips suddenly you see many whites having operations to enhance their lips, something we have naturally. You know the Culture War proponents and their supporters are not happy about that situation.

American's subliminal messengers will say that conscious expressions of African People are not commercial nor are they acceptable to the silent majority of whites in America.

If an African in America or an African-American goes afoul of what ever they feel is appropriate, they will feel an attempt to reach him or her, to pull them down, to divide and conquer or to out-right conquer them. You may even be told that you won't make up the corporate or career ladder maybe. Or, you maybe knocked off by some reorganization plan or even face lay off.

No matter what happens to you as a conscious African-American you must stay true to yourself and your people, work hard and keep the faith and continue to be whom you are and who we are. Ultimately, if America scorns you, please do not scorn yourself. Your dignity and mine, our soul and our essence belongs to us a people and we are not for sale. Our soul and essence belongs to us not Corporate America or the Culture War promoting neo- conservative right-wingers or left-wingers.

The irrational fear that is the foundation of white supremacy is based on the fact that 90% of the population of the world is African. Asian, Latin and South American or non-white. The irrational fear that the 90% will some how seek to wipe out the 10% is so totally irrational especially in view of the fact that all or the greatest amount of nuclear weapons have white fingers on the trigger. I hope that America too with its powerful business corporate elite and its right wingers particularly will be inspired to kill off its irrational racist fears and stop trying to be the world police trying to control the world to keep it ripe for multinational and transnational exploitation.

The Culture War including their media propaganda seeks to delete our African essence and replace it with apple pie. While we want or should think enough of ourselves to demand our legitimate reparations which we deserve for the unpaid work of our ancestors and for being victims of racial discrimination police brutality, disempowerment actions, relocations redevelopment plans and other forms of political oppression such as pole taxes and major road blocks to election voter registration.

Separate but unequal schools and many unpunished killings of African-Americans by the KKK and other neo-conservatives have been swept under the rug of history. Yet we as African people in Babylon 400 years remain as strong inside as our brothers and sisters all over the African world. Stand up we must today, tomorrow and in the future. Stand united and we can withstand the force of the cultural war proponents and other white American racists' neo-conservatives and outright white supremacists that despise our African ways of looking at our lives. Those folks really don't like us and will do anything they can to block our legitimate interests and rights. Stand up united and we can show ourselves what we can achieve together.

In the midst of the cultural war against our people by the stealth type oppressors we should stand up for ourselves. We should support conscious poet's, workers, Black Survivors, fathers, mothers, sisters and brothers, writers, painters, thinkers, great grand parents, grand parents, youth, children, baby boomers, scholars and others of us who promote visions of liberation for us; as a people. I hope these poems spoken and written words inspire as well as give you all visions of our liberation as well as struggle for liberation in the belly of the beast, we call America. I also hope we can spark a rethink in our circles and transform the crabs in a bucket mentality we see too much of today back to the active and activists coming together of our people and all progressive people to build a new politics of liberation that recognizes the new demographics in America and the world.

Table of Contents

Acknowledgements.. iii
Editorial Note iv
Release A Black Dove Of Peace vi
One Percent Greed ix
Foreword..xiii

History to Destiny Through Afrocentric Poetry..........................1
A Poem for Chinwe..2
No More Human Sacrifice 4
No Justice, No Peace 6
When Freedom is Won...7
Reparations 9
Black is Beautiful...11
So Much More 12
Wisdom of the Ages 13
The Fifth Century 14
Breathing While Black...15
Love of Learning 17
Inspiration...18
Love Is...19
Street People (And The Powers That Be)................................20
African Madness...21
Mashing Up My People..22
African Griot..23
Floating Down the Nile..24
African Patriots...25
Another African American..26
Uprising 27
The First Bullet Hit 28

Live Strong...30
Time Come...32
In These Hard Times...34
It Was A Sad Day..35
Until We Unite With Self Love 37
Feeling Run So Deep...38
Boots on Their Feet...40
Stereotypes 41
Racial Brothers..43
Stand Tall..45
A Poem Is..47
Free Mumia Abu-Jamal..49
George The Executioner...51
Racial Profiling..53
Accountable 55
Juneteenth 2003..57
A Poem for My Mother...59
Make it Stop 61
Unite Black Family...63
The Irony of It All 64
Pullback, Don't Attack..66
Pretty African Lips 68
Fela* Lived 69
Get Through 71
When Brothers?...72
Journey of Life 74
God Will Make a Way...76
Eye Candy in Atlanta 77
Why It Gotta Happen like That?.................................78
Welcome Black History 88 80
Unity Thang..82
Tribute to Langston Hughes..84
Tribute To All African Women 85
Larry D. Lumpkin...87
Hard Times II 89
Who Are We 90

Onward Into 91 92
Learn Our History 94
Tell Me I am Not A Dreamer 95
Before There Was Any History: 96
The Last Paper Poet 97
African-American History 98
Constructive Engagement 99
The Blacks Have-Not 100
Cousins 102
The Richness of a Culture..103
Flock Together...104
African People are Beautiful..105
The Moderates and the Militants................................106
Four Icons for Liberation: 107
A Poem Untitled 109
Youth Suicide Among Blacks......................................111
Stop That Bleaching 113
Stop The Killing..114
Soul Truth 115
Juneteenth Day 116
Young Blacks 118
Unity Thang..119
In Babylon 121
Same Old Song 122
Salute 123
Red, Black and Green..125
Reason 127
African Gin 128
African Palm Wine 130
Africa 131
Africa's Call 132
Let the Love Flow..133
All Across America 135
Black Roots Black Youth 136
Homeless Hotel...137
Speak Jazz Please Part 2 138

Racial Brothers 140

Love Is Part 2 142

People's Love 144

No More Unjust Wars 145

Senators and Diplomats 147

Afroan Unity 149

Rise and Win 151

Over Qualified/It Sho' Is Funky 152

Jim Crow Needs A Beating 153

Rise Again 155

Black California 156

It's A Black Thang: You Could Not Understand 157

A Poem for Dr. Jocob Crawford 158

My Dream 159

Red, Black and Green II 160

Celebrating Our Culture 161

Off Your Backs 163

Frisco Blues 164

Who Are the Afroans 166

Another Brother Has Been Shot 167

It Couldn't be Done (Run Jessie Run) 168

History of Our Struggle 170

Healing 172

If We Could? 174

Fighting in the Streets 176

I'm Proud 177

Black on Black Crime 179

We Are Together 180

Lagos Remembered 181

This Is Your Ancestors 183

African People Are Beautiful 184

Beauty is Soul Deep 185

Life is Love 186

Tribute to Our Family 188

Black Peace and Black Power 190

We Gone Be Free 191

The Chains Are On Our Mind 192
Thousands of Afroans 193
Reaganomic Blues 194
I Salute Marvin Gaye 195
Black Woman, You are a Poem 197
Brothers Killing Brothers..199
Identity to Those Ashamed of our Name 200
Stop Police Brutality..201
Raid on the Treasury 203
Spontaneous January 1984 205
Extermination 206
Freedom, Freedom, Freedom 207
Class 5 A Unity Rap 208
Intimidation...209
For You And Me..211
I Saw Them 212
Who Are We? 214
In Sweet Benin 216
A Day in June 218
Benin Arrival..219
Expression 220
All Across America 221
Tree of Life...222
On African Land 224
Chimarenga...225
Become Yourself 226
Dedicated to Young African-Americans 227
Jet Ride With a Sister 228
A Luta Continua 229
Benin Arrival..230
Journey to the Motherland 231
Calling on Our Ancestors...232
African Moon...233
Airport in Benin...234
Happy Kwanzaa 83-84 235
We Are the Unsung Heroes 236

Writing For Eternity 238
Feeling Good in Africa 239
As I am 241
The Irony of it All 242
Love Your Flavor 244
God Give Um Freedom 245
Continuously 246
Peace to the Motherland 247
There is a Poem 248
Whence We Came 249
Words of Inspiration 250
Free Palestine 251
When it All 252
The Faces of Africa 253
Get Through 254
Great God 255
Inspiration for Liberation 256
Rise Up Mighty People 257
There is Poetry 258
Liberation Blues 260
Oakland in 2002 261
There is Poetry 263
There is Poetry: Part 2 265
Why Discriminate? 266
Whence We Came 267
My People What Do You Say 268
The Beauty of a Sister 270
Don't Sing the Blues for Me 272
I Don't Like All I See 273
Let My People Go 274
Their Rhythms? Our Rhythms 275
Tight Jeans 277
Black Liberation or White Supremacy: 278
Black is Black 280
Rough Days for Me 281
Thank God for Melanin 282

Liberate Black History..283
Afroan Patriots 285
Black History Goes On 286
The Spirit of Africa..288
The Spirit of Africa..290
My Beautiful Wife..291
Nothing 292
I am A Dissident 293
Walk Together My People..294
I Know You Know Why...296
Son of Africa 297
Waiting for You..300

History to Destiny Through Afrocentric Poetry

March with me
on a journey
from our history
to our destiny
through these pages
of Afrocentric poetry

March together as we
toward liberty
free of brutality
to our destiny

From the atrocity
of our history
We march on
toward a new century

Slavery is an
atrocity
But we march on
to our destiny

Our destiny you see
In this century to be
free from police brutality
winning reparations
and enjoy the fruitful economy
until the day we are truly free.

A Poem for Chinwe

Chinwe was tall, plump and sweet
When met her
She knocked me off my feet

She was 100% Nigerian
Born in America
Raised in Nigeria
I met her studying in America.

Chinwe experienced Biafra
A native of Nkwerre
When I traveled to Nigeria
Chinwe was beside me.

Chinwe spoke broken, some Yoruba and Ibo
Chinwe's State was Imo.
Chinwe had a proud walk
And a pretty smile, as we would talk.

We got married
And life took us on a ride
We flew to Africa
Sitting side by side.

We traveled
Through out Nigeria
By car bus taxi and air.

Chinwe was with me
We lived in the city of Benin
Chinwe was my wife
And Chinwe was my queen.

Falling sick while
Pursuing a Ph.D.
When you left
You took apart of me.

Dedicated to Chinwe Amechi Uzoma Johnson-Redd (9/19/52 to 5/31/85).
Written in early September 2000.

No More Human Sacrifice

The USA
is a savage State
with Human Sacrifice
A Black man's fate

And the brutality
of this racist country
is the death penalty
applied unfairly

Murder by the state
is Human Sacrifice, like ancient rites
when we have o rights and oppressive plights

The state killed
Shaka Sankofa,
his family name
Gary Graham

Lock them up
Take them out
The Final solution
cause we have no clout

Sankofa today
No more tomorrow
Work harder for Mumia now
And avoid blood and sorrow

Free Mumia Abu Jamal
Stop their barbaric acts
Stop Human Sacrifice
Don't let it happen twice

Human Sacrifice
In a savage and racist state
Economic bondage and sacrifice
NO! our freedom we must take

Dedicated to Shaka Sankofa and Mumia Abu Jamal.

No Justice, No Peace

No Justice, No Peace
Southern Mississippi, Dearborn
West, north or East
Get fired up
Don't take it no more
Get Fired up
Don't take it no more

The murder of Blacks
must surely stop
by White civilians
and by the white cop
Stop the deadly chokehold
or watch vengeance unfold

There is a price
White America must pay
for slavery and lynching yesterday
and the murders
of this present day

And you better know
you are building up a rage
Call yourself a leader of the free
on a world stage

Remember Diallo and Brother Louima
MLK, Marcus and Malcolm X
Remember the mother's tears
Remember the modern hypocrisy
In the so-called leading democracy.

When Freedom is Won

When misery is all we see
You may not see our coming victory
When oppression has the rush on

When they insult us
When they curse us or cuss us
When they tell us our sun won't shine
When they kill us, that is a crime

No matter the intensity
make sure you see
The day will surely come
When freedom is won

When you are
In their captivity
Fired from a job
Or in a new slavery

Hanging, hanging
from a tree
Or victimized
By police brutality

When they say
You must bow down
When the rollers try
To make us frown

When they round us up
Or hold us down
Make sure, make sure
The vision is found

Because the day
Will surely come
When our people's freedom
Is Won.

Reparations

Part 1

To all of those
who died from violence
to all of those
sho suffered in silence
To those still living
to those who are dead
to those of us terrorized
to those unafraid.

Part 2

To those who sat
peacefully in Africa
To those stolen
in a village raid
to those raped
to those played
to those who suffered
on the middle passage
To our ancestors
who worked and
were never ever paid.

Part 3

To those captured
and treated like a slave
to those who died
in an unmarked grave
To those who suffered
down through the years
to those who suffered
and those with fears
to those in jail
where the system failed
To those of us Africans
America impelled
to those of us
they shot down
to those of us
some lost, some found.

Part 4

To us Black survivors
We must be paid
Reparations
Hear what I said!

For all the years
and white oppression
Justice demands reparations,
A white concession!

Black is Beautiful

Black is Beautiful
And it is so beautiful
To be black

Say it Black is beautiful
And it is so beautiful
To be Black

Marcus Garvey came
From Jamaica in 1917
To teach us Black is Beautiful
And to give us the Red, Black and Green

When Marcus came
We were ashamed
Lynched and hated
Oppressed in need of progress

Black is Beautiful
And that is a fact
Black is beautiful
It is beautiful to be Black

This is not a put down
Of the color of any other
We say this with pride
To our self, sister and brother

Black is beautiful
It is so beautiful
To be Black
And that's a fact.

So Much More

We can give
Each other the pleasure
And treat each
Like valuable treasure

Be that virtuous woman
And I'll be your great man
And together we can
Walk through life
Hand in hand

You can be my wife
We can be lovers and friends
As long as we are
the ones that win

We can open that door
And have so much more
WE can make our life
Just like paradise.

Dedicated to Ese Ohe Mamodu.

Wisdom of the Ages

The wisdom of
the ages is
the knowledge of God

Wisdom and knowledge
provides a way forward
when we are moving toward
real liberation
and reparations
for the African-American Nation

Wisdom is our spear
Knowledge, self-knowledge
Is our bullet
Truth is dear
Reason is our compass
Reparations is our focus

Unite we must
Primarily among us
To make America just
To all of us

But we also must
Unite us
For the love.

The Fifth Century

This is the fifth century
since we were captured
and forced into slavery

This is the fifth century
without reparations
for you and me

This is the fifth century
since we were kidnapped
by the slave master enemy

This is the fifth century
since the middle passage
when we were ravaged

This is the fifth century
since we arrived from Africa
brought in chains to America

But in the fifth century
we are going
to be free

In this fifth century
liberation
for you and me

In this fifth century
of captivity, no more misery
Black Folks
TAKE YOUR LIBERTY!!!

Breathing While Black

One Day
a brother was arrested
for breathing
while Black

A sister
was arrested
for driving
while Black

Too many times
It's just like that
When our folks are arrested
for breathing while Black

Ahmadu Diallo
Murdered and that's a fact
Because one morning
he was walking while Black

We all know
someone
We know it's
a fact

Arrested for
no good reason
driving while Black

And a Haitian Brother Louima
was subjected to an attack
Assaulted with a stick
Living while Black

Another brother is
about to be jacked
and his only crime
Breathing while Black

Walking while Black
Talking while Black
Running while Black
Thinking while Black

Driving while Black
Working while Black
Living while Black
Breathing while Black.

Love of Learning

It is my education, I'm earning
I am learning
Not misbehaving
Because I am creating

New ways to
Love learning
In new ways
Respect I am earning

From my fellow students
Who watch me study
I love to work
With a buddy!

I love to learn
To make my mind strong
So I am going
To get my learn on.

We love to learn
And sing our song
To make our mind strong
We are going to learn
And we will be strong.

Dedicated to all elementary school students.

Inspiration

Written by
Inspiration
writing without
Hesitation
Writing about
Situation
And our need
For liberation
Writing about
What I see
Writing about
What it be
Writing and rhythm
Writing my
Observations
Writing for my nation's
For my
Liberation!!!

Love Is

Love is bittersweet
Knocks one off their feet
Love is like a sugar beat

Don't blame love
For the misery
Don't blame love
For the pain we see

It's the lack
Of love you see
That causes
The world's misery

Do what you can
To make it better
Only goodness will make
The world last forever

Love is strong
Even the mighty see

Love is provided
By our loving God
We can spread love around
Share it and rise
Or let our world down

Love can grow
Between man and wife
Love is the strongest
force In this life.

Street People
(And The Powers That Be)

Street people of the new depression
Products of the new depression
Old poverty, a new expression
Can the opulent powers that be
Open their eyes and see

This shocking new reality
Modern people on their feet
Sleeping in their car
Sleeping on the street

Steaks are served
In a North Beach suite
While those destitute
Have to deal with the street

Where is the aid for the homeless?
And the guaranteed income
Or must the street explode
Before the battle is won

And the powers that be
Are living graciously
Because the oppressed, unequal
Because the oppressed, unequal

Are beautiful street people?
Who will ever forgive?
The selfish powers that be
The street people
Survive in poverty.

African Madness

African Madness
Cause so much sadness

A brother with a gun
Is running wild
He's so mad
He could kill a child

African Madness
Black on Black crime
Cause so much sadness
All the time

A brother shot Hugh Mondale
brothers shot Malcolm X
African madness
Causes so much sadness

Mad mad mad
Mad mad mad
Mad and madness
African madness

What we must realize
If we are to thrive

With Black self hate
We knock at hell's gate
With Black togetherness
We heal African Madness.

Mashing Up My People

Look at the KKK
Look at the CIA
Smashing up my people
Mashing up my people

Look at the FBI
You know the racist
Are riding high
As my oppressed people cry

Can you see the unemployed?
They won't stop till we're destroyed
So many brothers in custody
Who want to be free?

Talking about the real story
It is the shame of Old Glory
Smashing up my people
Mashing up my people

There is counter intelligence
The Blacks are under surveillance
They ordered the death of Malcolm
Open your eyes and see them

Smashing up my people
Mashing up my people.

African Griot

I am an African griot
With a poem
Pouring out of
My Black hand

Moving through
A Journey called life
Living on after
The death of my first wife

I am an African messenger
In life, I am a passenger
I am a time traveler
I am a lie shatterer

I am simple and complex
I am single and vexed
I am near the top
I cannot stop

The knowledge I must drop
To germinate on the spot
I am an African Griot.

Floating Down the Nile

Floating Down The Nile
Floating for a while
Floating with a smile
Floating so high
Like floating in the sky

Floating down the Nile
Altitude one mile
Floating down the Niger
Floating together and higher

Floating down the Zambezi
Floating down the Congo
Floating towards the Limpopo.

African Patriots

African patriots
Versus African despots
The battle is very hot
As patriots grab for the top

African despots are puppets
With foreign connections in their pockets
African people want their patriots
To save Africa from imperialist plots

While our patriots
Guard the people's money
The despots are filling all their pockets
Oppression of Africa must stop
Patriots grab for the top.

Another African American

What happened to
The young brother
Unidentified
His murder
Unjustified!!!!!!!!
The community
Is horrified!!!!!!
Cause just like
Apartheid
Another brother
Has just died!!!!!
We do not
Know his name
We do know
It is a shame
Apprehension
Was not their game
Cause they shot first
Which is totally insane
What happened to
the young brother?????
He was shot!!!!!!!
In a parking lot
Cause they said
He did not stop
When ordered by a shooting cop
What happened to the young brother?????
He was murdered!!!!!!!!!!!!!!!!!!!!!!!!!!!!!!

Uprising

Uprising in Afroa's heart
Uprising gonna tear it all apart
Do you know what it's about?
Uprising cause we're busting out

Uprising in Tennessee
Uprising in Miami
Against a white conspiracy
Cause we want to be free

Uprising against a closed door
Too many of us are just too poor
Do you know what we are fighting for?
Cause we can't take no more.

The First Bullet Hit

The First Bullet Hit
And the eyeball split
Then blood started flowing
Death bit by bit

Cause you fired at him
Your brother named Jim
Who used to live next door?
Outside a local store

So you warned your homie
Stay away from my turf

But your homie said
He is not scared
And your gang banging buddies
Said shoot him till he's dead

When you caught Jim
And fired at his eye
And his blood flowed
You realized he would die

But you say you don't care
Really you are unaware
Now you are scared
And in despair
Cause of the gang-banger's dare

Jim died on your turf
His mom cried in the dirt
His buddies swore
To make your blood flow

But do you ever ask why?
We got to fight till we die
Instead practicing unity
In our own community

Do you ever ask why?
They laugh while we cry
Cause we treat each other
Like an enemy
While white society
Oppresses you and me

That self-destruction song
Play it all day long
We are committing suicide
Self assisted Black genocide
We are committing self-suicide
Self assisted Black genocide

We could like with pride
Instead of self assisted genocide
Cause black on black love
Is much better than
Black on Black crime.

Live Strong
Dedicated to and written for my People (A Kwanzaa poem)

A year is promised to no one
One never knows if day will come
Happily we live on
Truth is we live strong

We refused slavery
We've displayed bravery
Must control our community
And live in unity and harmony

In the coming year
Our numbers get larger
If more of us unite
We'll get stronger

Just as sure as
Racism is wrong
We got to unite
So we can be strong

Right on Right on
We got to live strong
And if they kill one of us
We must kick up the dust

Our struggle continues
Year after year
Cause we refuse
A life based on fear

Brothers and Sisters
United together
We must be united
Together forever.

Time Come

What are you going to do?
When the time has come
If we do not unite
We will be on the run

Black folks will you learn
The value of unity
When will you learn?
To agree on one strategy

When you least expect
Your time may come
With no strategy
You will be on the run

Will you learn?
National Liberation must be earned
Cause the time may come
We will be on the run

Afroans Black
Victims of hypocrisy
Fighting ugly Americans
So we can be free

What will we do?
The day may come
We can unite
Or, we'll be on the run

Running from the Nazi
From the KKK
From a racist policeman
In the land of Uncle Sam

Running from disunity
From ugly Americans
Running from the man
In the land of Uncle Sam.

In These Hard Times

In these hard times
Police committing murderous crimes
Some take bribes, we pay the fines
In these hard times

In these hard times
A job is hard to find
Unemployment can blow your mind
The day is bleak yet the sun shines
In these hard times

Hard times for my brothers
Hard times for my sisters
Hard times for my people
Trying to be equal

The day is bleak
Yet the sun shines
They are killing my kind
In these hard times.

It Was A Sad Day

This poem was read on television in Benin City in 1979 with a Nigerian drummer who beat a tune that sad it was a sad day in the Yoruba language.

It was a sad day
when they took
All of the Blacks away
Smiles on their face
Cause Blacks finally
To be put in their place.

It was a sad day
After 400 years of slavery
We finally realized
We were not free in white society
As we were rounded up
And taken away
On that sad day.

We regretted
Spent wolf tickets
Sold the other day
And being cool it boys
It didn't help anyway

In four hundred years
Of suffering death and tears
We never thought
They would do us that way
Until that sad day

There was laughter
In America's air
Whites celebrated everywhere
Time had come to pass
There would be no Blacks at last

Revolutionary Black leaders
Just the day before
Said we better get organized
Or we won't exist any more

We never realized
We'd feel the pain
Of not being organized
In such a surprising way
The very next day.

The sky was lit by helicopters
with illuminating lamps
They were taking us
To the concentration camps!!!!

Until We Unite With Self Love

We'll see rivers of Blood
Until we unite with self love
We'll see Rivers of Black blood
Until we unite self love

We've been running like a river
From oppression in this land
We'll be running like the river
Hear me Black Man

From white atrocity to black atrocity
To white philosophy
Racism against the Black Man/Woman
Is a stain on this land?

We'll see rivers of blood
Rivers of our own blood
Like a snowballing flood
Until we find self-love.

Feeling Run So Deep

FEELINS RUN SO DEEP
IN MY African soul
My people suffer
In the land of gold

Feeling run deep
From my mind to my soul
I speak of the Africans
They bought and stole.

Feelings run deep
Through to my soul
Bound by the skin
Of my ancestors of old.

Feelings run deep
In this Black Man's soul
Concern for my people
Young and old.

When feelings rise up
To my mind
They send a chill
Through my spine.

I feel the day
I feel the night
I see the need
Africans must fight

Feelings run so deep
In my soul
My people have suffered
In the land of gold

No respect, benign neglect
Bakkke, Nazi, Zebra are
But a code
Oppression of Blacks is the mode

Some know the feelings
Those who don't behold
Feelings run so deep
In my African soul.

Boots on Their Feet

The kkk no longer wears sheets
In uniforms and boots on their feet
Ronald Reagan is the grand goon
Who's got to go soon?
The kkk used to exclusively for us
Now Reagan sent them to Grenada
with M16"s
Can you hear our brothers screams
T
Done scared all N'S
Those around here
Got to find some more
Far or Near
White sheets hiding white terror
Marines and the Army in Grenada
With orders to shoot to kill
just for the kicks and the thrill
You can kill a revolutionary
But not the revolution.
Till we take Black Liberation
There is no other solution
The kkk needs no sheets
the grand goon
Is in the white house
but he'll be gone soon
his karma is doom
his destiny is gloom
We don't like is tune
and he will go soon.

Stereotypes

Stereotypes of
The powers that be
About the extended
African family

They say we are different
From each other
When we are
Sister and brother

They call Palestinians
Israeli Arabs
They are myths
That must be shattered

They call Pacific Africans
Melanesians
But All Africans
Share melanin

They Call
Caribbean Africans
West Indians,
We are friends
and we are kin

They called us
Colored and Negroes
We are African-Americans
Not foes but friends

Around the globe
We live, behold, no fraud
Africa for us Africans
Those at home
Those abroad.

Racial Brothers

Are you Edo?
Can you speak Ibo?
Who is Oyibo
Tell me if you know

Are you a Hausa Man?
Are you a Kanuri Man?
Let us all join together
We are racial brothers

Hey brother man
Are you from Yorubaland?
Are you a Shona
Are you from Zululand?

We Are Racial brothers
Come on Black People let's pull together
Talking to my racial sisters and brothers
Come on Black People let's get it together

I know you been robbed
By some crazy brothers
I've been there too
Why do we harm each other?

Are you a West Indian?
Are you from the Caribbean?
We are blood brothers
We are racial brothers

Blood much thicker than water
And brothers that's a fact
And who needs unity more
Than my fellow Blacks

We are racial brothers
We look like no others
From Black Fathers and Black Mothers
We are racial sisters and brothers.

Stand Tall

Hear the call
We must stand tall
Ignore the call
and see our downfall
Better we stand tall
united we stand
when we hear the call
all turfs together
brothers and sisters
united forever
Better we stand tall
If you make
another brother fall
you ignore our
Ancestor's call
and you may face
Judgment day
for ignoring this call
and acting that way
Unless you are deaf
and you can't hear
or if you are dumb
and you can't think
better open your eyes
you better not blink
control yourself
when you drink

open your ears
and hear the call
you know we must
stand very tall
united we stand
Divided we fall.

A Poem Is

A poem is strong
Short or long
It can stop
Or go on and on

A poem reflects
Feelings so strong
A poem can be
A liberation song

A poem can
Cross the road
And lift up
A heavy load

A poem can
Open a mind
A poem can
Lift up my kind

A poem can reach
The pit of our soul
A poem is
A story told

A poem is great
A poem is grand
A poem is like
Our African Homeland

A poem can drop
Knowledge from a tree
A poem can end
Our modern misery

A poem can state
Feelings that are great
This poem is for
You and me.

Free Mumia Abu-Jamal

Hey people
one and all
get together
and free Mumia-Jamal

There was a conspiracy
Up north in Philly
They lined Jamal
Against the wall

And shot him down
Trying to take him out
Every one hear the call
We must free Brother Jamal

There was no trial
and no real adequate defense
Another conspiracy
and that's common sense

Now they have our brother
on their death row
Hold on people
Don't let our brother go

Listen people
one and all
Let's work together
and free Mumia-Jamal

Give Mumia Abu-Jamal
A brand new trial
or William J. Clinton
What about a Presidential Pardon?

Abu's people and family
want to see him free
while racists in Philly
You know he is not guilty!!

We saw from the helicopter
Video of blue corrupt rage
We know there is a conspiracy
up north in old Philly

Come on people
heed the call
Let's work together
to free Mumia-Jamal

Come on people
shout out aloud
You know he's not guilty
Set Mumia Free

Come on my people
Join the crowd
You know he is not guilty
Set Abu Free

Come on people
Let us work together
You know he's not guilty
SET JAMAL FREE.

George The Executioner

King George III
of colonial era England
was a slave-trading bastard
spreading racist terror

Now Prince George Bush
after 132 killings
has earned the title
George the executioner

George is the killer
running for President
but can you smell the smell of
his murderous scent?

He has murdered
a women and many a man
Despite no evidence
George murdered Shaka Sankofa

Prince George
the murderer
the mad executioner

killed 132
while only
governor

Murderer executioner
we smell your scent
We pray you do not
become our President

Murder by injections
human sacrifice
he has done it more than once

Texas is
a savage state
oppression there is
a BLACKMAN'S fate
where they dragged
BROTHER BYRD to death
to join the KKK

And now he wants
our vote
May his mad plans
go up in smoke

How can we vote?
for a mad executioner
killed more than 132 prisoners
while only a governor
and no public defender

132 killings
a royal brute's killing spree
Human sacrifice in the
so-called land of the free.

Racial Profiling

Racial Profiling
is nothing but discriminating
Racial Profiling is targeting
and a very evil sin

Racial profiling
Breathing while Black
And if you're young
you know that it is a fact

Racial Profiling
when we walk in their stores
Racial profiling
as soon as we walk in the doors

And we Black Men
are public enemy #1
The usual suspect
It's our rights we week to protect

Racial Profiling
as we're walking down the street
Racial profiling
In our own community

Racial Profiling
North, East, South and West
Racial profiling
what a democratic mess

Racial profiling
New York and New Jersey
Racial Profiling
throughout this country

Racial profiling
and police brutality
Oppression politicians don't see
Oppression of African-Americans in totally

About racial profiling
White folks it better end!!!
racial profiling,
an ugly American sin

We'll be forever divided
When police are too excited
END EXCESSIVE FORCE
AND RACIAL PROFILING.

Accountable

In a thousand years
Or a thousand nights
You could not repay us
For slavery's stolen rights

In a thousand moons
Or a thousand noons
Even if you atoned
With a thousand sorrowful tunes

For slavery America must
Hold it accountable
Or it's promises
Are extremely doubtable

A thousand years
Could not erase
Our ancestor's tears.

Or the scars
On their backs
Or their slave masters brands
On their arms and hands

How did they feel?
When brothers were killed
Or beaten near dead
In the master's field

When wives and sisters
Were taken and shaken
There was no love
There was raping

America, hold yourself
Accountable
Pay reparations
Or your pillars, your democracy
Are extremely doubtable.

Juneteenth 2003

Drumbeats and barbecue
in the air
my people thick
here and there

This is a Juneteenth affair
celebrate us
if you dare
and our liberation shows you care

Sun is shining
our folks are thick
not one brother
is throwing a lick

Kids are playing
across the street
the smells are smelling
oh so sweet

Eye candy everywhere
look, enjoy
but please don't stare

Music too
in the air
if you missed it
you'd whish you were here

It was 138 years ago
when they let
the last
brothers and sisters go

Rappers are rapping
Jazz is playing
the funk is on
our people are swaying

Youth are playing
Basketball
Its Juneteenth and
we are standing tall

Juneteenth on Fillmore Street
music is great, the beat
and the children are jumping
like the hot sun is humping

Kids riding on the scooters
its getting hot in here
on the microphone
and beautiful colors
of people with black a tone.

A Poem for My Mother

My mom is love
From God above
Tough, compassionate, soulful
Spiritual love
My mom gave me
The ultimate gift
And so many ancestral gifts
And when my head was bowed
So many inspirational lifts
When I was young
Mom gave me knowledge
And wisdom
Mom also gave me
A part of God's kingdom
And mom gave this love
To all seven of us
And never complained
About the burdens of us
And is loved by all of us
You can look
At all seven of us
And see mom's beautiful hand,
Tough and sweet.
African-American Women
From North Little Rock,
Arkansas (Tieplant area)
Mom you are my roots
My connection to my past

My link to our African ancestor
And giver of my future
Because with no past,
There is no future
Momma, you are God's gift
To all seven of us.

Make it Stop

All over the
African-American Nation
We must unite
To seek liberation
Cause Black on Black crime
Is a shame!
When freedom
Is the name
Of the game

Stop the crazy killing
Or continue the pain
We're feeling
Risking our destiny
Dieing over community

All over our nation
Black on Black killings
On the rise
All over our nation
Hear mothers and sisters cries

And brothers
We can make the killing stop
Practice peace in the hood
On every block
Stop killing your brother man

This is our people's demand
So we can assassinate
Discrimination
And take our liberation
And take our piece of the rock
In this white man's nation
So brothers on every block
Come together
And make the killing stop!!!

Unite Black Family

Unite Black Family
so we can meet
our liberated destiny

we will never be free
with this much disunity
unity is a must
in our black family

unity for our people
with a history not equaled
unity for our nation
unity for liberation

Unity for survival
unity with a rival
we're strong in fights
not to have all our rights

United Black family
Unite African family
so we can meet
a liberated destiny

Please let there be
Black solidarity
In the Black Community
and the black Family.

The Irony of It All

The irony of it all, you rise and you fall
The Blacks were standing tall
Until our downfall

In Egypt, Zimbabwe
In the Congo and Songhay
In the Black mainstream
Do you know what I mean?

Whether we are short
Or very very tall
The irony of it all
You rise and you fall

America, South Africa
Caribbean and Pacifica
White feet stampede
On Black hopes and dreams

The scars are deep
What's yours you keep?
It's white domination
Versus Black Liberation

The irony of it all
In Zimbabwe and Songhay
Black Men stood tall

In Egypt and the Congo
Black Women stood tall
Until a historical decline and fall
That is the irony of it all

Blacks all over the world
Some take orders from whites
Blacks all over the world
Fighting for our rights

The Black race ruled our destiny
Until our down fall
The irony of it all
You rise and you fall
United We Stand—Divided We Fall.

Pullback, Don't Attack

Instead of feeding and clothing the homeless
And building a warm place to stay
George Bush wants
To occupy and takeover
IRAQ today

The people are saying
Take care of the problems right here
But deaf George Bush
Has oil in his ear
And he can't hear

Eliminate racism, poverty and ignorance
In the USA today
That is what the people say
But George Bush wants a war
Any—way

Sad to see a general
Act like a puppet
So sad to see Condelisa
Act like a Muppet

With the oil barrens
Pulling the string
And the whole world
Will feel the sting

Pull back from
This foolish attack
On the people
And the republic of Iraq

Pullback, don't attack
PULL BACK, DON'T ATTACK
PULL BACK, DON'T ATTACK
THE PEOPLE AND THE OIL OF IRAQ.

Pretty African Lips

I want to kiss you
But I can't
I want to touch you
A reality it may seam
But that's only a dream

A whole continent away
Wished I could touch you
The first thing this day
Yet you are far way

I want to kiss your lips
I wonder about you
From your laps, thighs and hips
I really want to kiss
Your pretty lips

So I'm writing this poetry
Stirred up by your picture
Thinking of your pretty lips
Wondering about your pretty hips.

Fela* Lived

When the ship was full
They put out to Sea
Headed for the Americas
And American Slavery

Yet the British
Turned the ship back
And everyone is put down
Or freed in Sierra Leone/Freetown

Fela's ancestors
Were in that group
They walked back to Nigeria
And founded Abeokuta

Fela, the social activist
And opponent of military government
The Africa 70 Band
Made the record 'Zombie'
Mocking the military man
And military government

Fela, the politician
Ran for the Presidency
In 1979
The Movement of the People Party was
On a radical frequency

Then came the Kala Kuta Republic
And Fela's Mom was killed
During an assault of the military man
And then came the Egypt 80 band

Fela created Afro beat
Fela was loved by the man
On the Street
Fela was a prominent opponent
Of Nigeria's military government

Fela died at sixty
The status quo's enemy
With 27 wife's
And radical legacy.

Fela Anikulapo Kuti (1938-1997)
was a Nigerian musician, arranger, producer and politician.

Get Through

I tried to call
You are not here
If your were here
This is what
I would say dear

I love talking to you
Longing for us to be near
In love
But distance I fear

What I really want
Is to bring you near
My beautiful dear
Can you hear?

Tried to call
But I couldn't get through,
This is what
I would say to you.

When Brothers?

When will the
The brothers get tired
of beating each other down
all over town

Fighting each other
in the flat lands
and Jack London Square
Fighting and killing clans

When will our brothers
get fired
of burying each other
Are we all sister and brother?

When will we stop?
drowning in each others blood
Aren't we made?
from the same precious mud?

When will our brothers
get tired
whatever happened
to "One Love"

When will the brothers
get tired
of killing each other
my brother?

When my brothers?
standing in each other's blood
when my brothers?
Made from the good black mud.

Journey of Life

The wisdom and
Knowledge of Life
Must be passed
To the youth
So they know
Our heritage
So they know
So they know the truth
In this journey called life
If you are single
Or if you have a wife
Cause, as you know
You got to go
With the righteous flow
Sometimes fast Sometimes slow
Get yourself a knife
Cut your slice of liberation
Unite our nation
Journey through
Stages and rights of passages
In life's carriage
Learn our history
of stolen rights
In this journey
Discover your purpose
Go deeper than
The surface
Make a contribution
That is profound
To our liberation

We must be
Unbound
The courage found to
Hear the sound
As we continue on
And try to get strong
In a committed way
This very day
In our journey called.

God Will Make a Way

Go will make a way
I will unite with a wife
soon one day
and we'll be on our way

Don't rush
the land is lush
open the door
of a blessing in store

She will be nice
and very sweet
she will be
the real deal

Soul sister
Black Queen
And I'll be
her Black king

And the day will come
we'll unite as one
We'll live together
live life and have fun.

Eye Candy in Atlanta

The girls and women
Are so pretty
In this
Chocolate city

So many pretty smiles
Dressed in the latest styles
And the sisters are very intelligent
Talking to a sister, is time well spent

In a city
That Blacks rule
And many folks
Go to school

And all the
Pretty faces
In so many
different places

On the streets
Clubs and malls
See pretty intelligent women
Not just pretty dolls

in the home of Coca Cola
and even Fanta
see all the eye candy
In the sisters of Atlanta.

Why It Gotta Happen like That?
(Code Switch)

Why it gotta
happen like that?
Why it gotta
happen like that?

You attack a person
In a skin that's Black

You are a KKK
Going to hang a Black today
wearing a sheet by night
and a uniform by day

You are a fellow Black
It is your brother you attack
Cause he is from another set
You fight or rat, tat, tat,tat

Why does it?
happen like that
Aren't we all Black?
Why it gotta happen like that?

Attacking your sister
You know she is pretty, feminine and Black
If you are a strong man
Why do you attack?

Why does it have
to happen like that
Can you cut a little slack?
To a person that is Black?

you got that brother
put in jail with no bail
He didn't hit you
but you're a jealous girl

Why it gotta happen
like that
Why do we
have to attack?

Why it gotta
happen like that
Why does it
have to happen
like that?

Welcome Black History 88

Welcome another year
Of our History
Which dates back
To the original story

Of the first people
From Eastern Africa
Who looked like you and me?
This is our history

Another year to battle
For African liberation
Freedom for our Black Nation
For all of Mother Africa: Black Emancipation

We will out live our oppressors
We will defeat those suckers
To racist police and the KKK
We say, every dog has its day

Cause we have a future to build
We must prepare for our field
Develop our mind
And learn to love our kind

So we can understand our mystery
So we can build our history
So we can establish our liberation
Unite and raise Black Nation

Rise up from degradation
Rise up from low self-esteem
Rise up lost younger generation
Raise up Black Kings, Black Queens

In a real year like 88
Please do not be a fake
Express how you really feel
And make Black history real

With our Black woman
By our side
And more love among our people
We will surely rise.

Unity Thang

If we are all in
The same gang
Then it's
A unity thang

Brothers and sisters
in our community
End the war
Practice more unity

26 caskets
Lined up at City Hall
26 killed in 24 months
Must more fall

To the young brothers
To the young men
Don't be a killer
Be a brother or a friend

Stop being a clown
Warring brothers
From the other
Side of town

Unless self destruction
is our function
One gang you see
It is a unity thang

To much blood is shed
Too many under fed
Too many oppressed
Too many dead

Too many mothers
Too many years
Too many sons killed
Too many tears

If we all in
The same gang
Then it's
A Unity Thang

Brother and sister
In our community
End the warfare
We need more unity.

Tribute to Langston Hughes
and All Other African-American Poets

You must have
Had spiritual inspiration
You must have felt
The pulse of liberation

You had to sit down
And Jot it down
On newspaper
Or whatever could be found

And through that rhyme
History was recorded in time
Telling stories
Of our oppressed people
Destined to be equal

You labored when
Many didn't dare
You wrote even though
Some didn't care

You wrote it down
And read it too
You did what
You had to do

And this is my tribute to you: (also dedicated to Ameri Baraka, Sonia Sanchez, Haki Madhubuti and Muta Baruka).

Tribute To All African Women

Some think
We're not it
Some think
We're not up to it

This is a tribute
To all Black Women
You've always been
Our very best friend

Sharing our identity
Walking with us through history
Walking out of slavery
Sharing our destiny

This is a tribute
To all African Women
You've always been
Our very best friend

Together we are family
We are not enemies
We are together
Like birds and bees

Every time we spoke
We are the same folk
You are the best lovers
For me and my brothers

Never ever forget
Please unite us together
All of us
Are sister and brother

This is a tribute
To all Black Women
You have always been
Our very best friend

You are
A Work of Art
You are
Queen of heart

You are
The roots we need
You are
The pillar of our creed

This is a tribute
To all African Women
Have always been
Our very best friend.

Larry D. Lumpkin

Brothers and Sisters
We are all Kin
Don't forget
Brother Larry Lumpkin

A dread brother
Cut his hair
The problem was
No employer cared

One day, Larry met
The undercover blue
They shot our brother
We know that's true

And left him outside
Just like genocide
So unjustified
To undignified

Show some concern
Show that you care
Show more self-love
Show that you're aware

Brothers and sisters
We are all kin
Don't forget
Brother Larry Lumpkin

He had rights
But they didn't care
Shot in cold blood
And then they left him there.

Hard Times II

Hard Times
Hard Rhymes
In the Rain
And the Sunshine
Ask God for mercy
Hold on Steady
When times are good
You will be ready
Tire is flat
Pockets are broke
Ask GOD for some
Better days will surely come.

Who Are We

Who are we?
Who are we?
Are we Negroes?
Are we Negroes?

No! No! No! No!
We are African people
We are African people

Brother can't you hear?
Sister can't you hear?
We are African people
We are African people

Who are we?
Who are we?
Are we colored people?
Are we colored people?

No! No! No! No!
We are African people!
We are African people!

Who are we?
Who are we?
Are we N's?
Are we N's?

No! No! No! No!
We are African people!
We are African people!

Brother can't you hear?
Sister can't you hear?
We are African people!
We are African people!

This Poem was written in 1968 or 1969
(Original Version)

Onward Into 91

Onward my people
Into 1991
Struggle for our rights
till the battle's won

Onward my people
keep making our history
Onward my people
Move toward our destiny

Walk over Uncle Sam
Beat down the Ku Klux Klan
Stop killing your brother man
Black skins, self love understand

Onward my people
Into 1991
It must be obvious
Self Destruction is no fun

Move on my people
Happy Kwanzaa to you
Onward into 1991
Self-love will get us through

Onward Black South Africa
Onward African-American
Onward through out the African world
Every Black man woman boy and gal

Onward my people
Into Tax year 1991
Struggling for our rights
Until our battle's won.

Learn Our History

Learn our History
Prepare for our destiny

Learn our success
Learn our mistakes

Learn our accomplishments
And our freedom movements

Learn the despair of disunity
Learn the fate of self-hate
Learn to love each other
Love your sister and brother

Learn our history
Prepare for our destiny
Learn to live in unity
In our black community

Learn about math and science
Learn and we all advance
Learn to love each other
So we can dance.

Tell Me I am Not A Dreamer

Tell me not that I am a dreamer
Cause I want my people free
Tell me not that I am crazy
Cause I want my liberty

My country tis thee
Land of modern slavery
From the big city
To the country

In this land of racism
They make my skin a prison
Blame the powers that be
And official police brutality

Tell me not that I'm a dreamer
Cause one day we will be free
Do not say we are crazy
Cause we want our liberty!!!!

This poem was written on the 28th day of December 1982. This poem was and is dedicated to Nevell Johnson whose killer was acquitted of all murder charges by an all white jury.

Before There Was Any History:
There Was African History
African History Month 1991

You know his name
was not George
In Kenya's
Oldavai Gourge

We are Adam and Eve
The original people
we are treated everyway
but equal

Yet there is one fact
about a skin that's black
Before there was any history
there was African History

Among the Olmecs
And in Papua, New Guinea
Deep in the Congo
Deep as you can go

By Mount Kilaminjaro
down in Soweto
up on Hunter's Point Hill
And down in the ghetto

Hot are the coals
In our deep dark souls
From the country
To our inner city.

The Last Paper Poet

I have written
many a poem
Every now and then
I share or show them

All of the poems
are written on paper
A paper poet
unafraid to show it

In a world
where rappers abound
and this old world
keeps turning around

But I write on paper
where I cut and shape
or make
poems I feel are great.

African-American History
Twelve Months a Year

Africa is old and new
We are too
With love there is
Nothing to fear
Celebrate our history
Twelve months a year

Our blood is old
Our blood is new
Our blood is preserved by
Dr. Charles Drew

We still love our
Okra and our greens
Our grits, our food and
Other African things

With our African roots
Our history is clear
However, we
Live right here

Keep the best
Of the old and the new
The solution is near
Celebrate African-American history
Twelve months a year.

Dedicated to all past and present Bret Harte Elementary School students.

Constructive Engagement

Constructive Engagement
Nuclear co-operation is nuclear aid
For Racist South Africa
Shame on racist America

Constructive engagement
Is collaboration?
As Azania rises
For Black Liberation

Implicit support
For racist Apartheid
Where the Black Women
Must run and hide

Constructive engagement
And economic aid
No political or other rights
And Black people are underpaid

constructive engagement
Is brotherly aid
When whites are free and
The black man: A slave.

Black South Africa achieved liberation and the right to vote in 1994

The Blacks Have-Not

Few haves
Too many have-nots
They oppress those
With Afro knots

Black resistance
Cover the distance
They kill Blacks
In the first instance

Too few have
Too many have-nots
They even oppress
Natty dread locks

Like crabs in a bucket
One may try to escape
Other crabs pull him back
Why do some Blacks act like that?

Every Black knows
We must unite Black souls
A divided race is a pity
And that is how it goes

A sinking ship
An unjust land
They use budget cuts
Against the Black Man

The whites have
We Blacks have not
For liberation we plot
Cause Oppression must stop

Let us fight our best
With what we got
They have
The Blacks have not.

Cousins

One brother
Shoots another
down
Cause they
Lived in
Another part
of town
But they
were cousins
You see
Who thought
They were
enemies
Because they
grew up in
different communities.

The Richness of a Culture

The Richness
Of a Culture
Let us behold
Lies within our soul

The richness
Of a culture
Is found in our History
Today it's in our identity

In the way
That we walk
In the way
That we talk

In the way
We express Love
In the way
We praise Jah above

The richness
Of our culture
Is found in Africa
We brought it to America

The richness
Of our culture
Is rooted in our family
You and me.

Flock Together

Groups of brothers and sisters
Fighting each other
When we are sisters and brothers
Fighting each other

When we should flock together
Taking the wrong turn
The pain will surely burn
Burning each other

When we should flock together
Cause a people without a vision
Will surely perish
or die in looking at television

Brothers killing and
beating each other down
And this happened all over town
We must make sure it never happens again

All my brothers
Let's try to be friends
So we can work together
So we can survive and thrive for now and forever

The Russians and Americans
All of them cooperate
We got to unite
so we can operate.

African People are Beautiful

African people have pretty eyes
African women have pretty thighs
African people have pretty lips
African women have pretty hips

African people on many trips
African people came on slave ships
African people dark to fair
African people have pretty hair

African people have a pretty nose
African people make pretty clothes
African people will never fade
Not the African people God made

African people have a developed mind
African people can be so kind
African people have pretty Black skin
African people we are all kin

African unity is wonderful
African unity is powerful
African people be truthful
Because African people are beautiful.

The Moderates and the Militants

The small fries and the elephants.
It is time we decide
To unite city and nation wide
Cause if you are big or small
And white racism has a fall
United Blacks will bounce so high
Higher than their golf balls
The militants and the moderates
Nationalists or Pan Africanists
Moderates and Black Socialists
Unite all of our activists.

Four Icons for Liberation:
Mandela, Marcus, Martin and Malcolm

Strong African
Political leaders
From Africa
To African-America

Mandela and Marcus
The vision of liberation
That is what you are

Malcolm and Martin
You too are
Strong leaders
And a freedom star

Icons for justice and liberation
Freedom fighters in every way
Because of your efforts
We are closer to Black freedom day

We are proud of you too
But we must go all the way
Make freedom real
On Black freedom day

Led by leaders past and present
And our people
Marching all the way
Uniting together for
Worldwide Black Freedom Day

Marching with the progressives
Of every color, race and nation
Marching for African Liberation
And World Liberation

For wise Black sages
A Black Liberation war rages
This, this is the
wisdom of the ages!

A Poem Untitled

I said I
would not write
more poems
then I heard
what happened?
in West Virginia
on N.P.R.
2 white youths
beat a Black Man to death
and then
ran over him
several times on
July 4, 2000
The murder of Blacks
Must stop
when it comes
to reparations
we are owed
a lot
How can I stop?
Is there a debate?
Is this a crime of hate?
Must this be our fate?
Must we be
the murdered and the murderer
we are already
a victim of your system
but until you know
we won't take it any more
don't call yourself

the leader of the free
when you kill us
while we are in misery of your
oppressive variety
of white elite society.

Dedicated to the family of the brother killed in north central West Virginia.

Youth Suicide Among Blacks

Dedicated to Gang Warriors.

Aids is going around
Please have no doubt
If you toss yourself up
You throw yourself out

Not just blaming youth
We all need the truth
We need a renaissance revival
To solidify black survival

Not Black on Black crime
Erupting all the time
Blacks killing Blacks
get the facts

Youth must be their own savior
From high risk behavior

In a time of low self-esteem
And oppression of the Black King/Queen
No Black studies in School
Only Greeks and Romans are cool

Self Love is near dead
As our elders live scared
Respect to elders unpaid
Cause self hate is widespread

How can we survive?
Our youth are headed toward suicide
Cause we are the most threatened
With life threatening genocide

Mighty African Youth
Do not March off to suicide
You are our only hope
If we are to survive

Kill Black on Black Crime
End gang warfare
Rekindle Black Pride
And we will surely survive.

Stop That Bleaching

Stop that bleaching
Do you hear, I am preaching
It is your brother speaking
Sisters stop that bleaching

Stop that bleaching
Leave that Blackness alone
Stop that bleaching
Shine on Black tone

Do not be mad
Cause I'm on your case
Fact of the matter is
You are betraying our race

Stop that bleaching
My sisters in America
A for real brother is speaking
To my sisters in Africa

Stop that bleaching
It is pure insanity
Black is beautiful
And oh so pretty

Stop that bleaching
Do you hear what I'm saying?
Stop that bleaching
Better hear what I'm preaching.

Stop The Killing

Stop Stop Stop
All this violence
Or surely our race
Will go down in silence

It is the death
of our race
It is a damned disgrace

Stop the violence
Stop the killing
Stop this pain
Our mothers keep feeling

Stop this fratricide
Brothers Killing brothers
And brothers killing sisters

Stop this useless killing
Stop the killing
We been dealing
Stop the killing
Start the Healing.

Soul Truth

I love your
Dark deep tone
And your light brown skin
Really turns me on

Love your
Hazel to dark eyes
Love your curves
And historically close ties

Love to see you while
I'm walking down the street
Really love to see you
Even if we do no speak

Dark and lovely
Light and out of sight
One race, one destiny
You know that's right

Springing from
A common root
Black Women are beautiful
And that's the soul truth

Juneteenth Day

Not yet liberated
On Juneteenth
Day Not Yet Uhuru
Talking about me and you

The day they say
They set slaves Free
Prove that by
You and me

Emancipation Day
They say
They set
The slaves free

Emancipation day
They say
they ended
the misery

But you tell me
truthfully
Can they prove that?
by you and me

We got emancipation
We are fighting for Black Liberation
Ending police brutality
And racial discrimination

We need self-love
And more love for our kind
If we work together
We can make our sun shine

We got emancipation
But we ain't free
No 40 acres
and no mule, do we?

We need unity
between you and me
If we really
Want to be free

Not yet liberated
On Juneteenth
Day Not yet Uhuru
Talking about you and me.

Young Blacks

Young Blacks
In America
Do you know
We come from Africa
To be Young Gifted and Black
Is where it's at
Do you know?
How we got here
And you still think
There's nothing to fear
When it's dog bites
Or hanging like kites
Put your sights
On fighting for our rights
To be Young Gifted and Black
Is where it's at
And that's a fact
Check out the wisdom of the ages
Our tradition and current situation
We need love
In our Black Nation
and Black Liberation.

Unity Thang

If we are all in
The same gang
Then it's
A unity thang

Brothers and sisters
in our community
End the war
Practice more unity

26 caskets
Lined up at City Hall
26 killed in 24 months
Must more fall

To the young brothers
To the young men
Don't be a killer
Be a brother or a friend

Stop being a clown
Warring brothers
From the other
Side of town

Unless self destruction
is our function
One gang you see
It is a unity thang

To much blood is shed
Too many under fed
Too many oppressed
Too many dead

Too many mothers
Too many years
Too many sons killed
Too many tears

If we all in
The same gang
Then it's
A Unity Thang

Brother and sister
In our community
End the warfare
We need more unity

In Babylon

Brothers and sisters
Under the sun
Stick together
in Babylon

As long as we
Are under the sun
We might as well
Unite as one

No need to kill
one another
When we can
Love each other

No love in a Babylon
Normal life is corruption
Babylon eats up our youth
And smiles like bitter fruit

Brothers and sisters
Under the sun
Stick together
In Babylon.

Same Old Song

The same unholy story
Hypocrisy in old glory
Same old song
Same old sad song

The keep saying
Don't you worry
But we are tired
Of the same old story

Oppression is misery
My country tis of thee
My people are not free
In this racist country.

Salute

Salutations
To all Black Nations
I Salute
All Black People

If they scorn you
Please don't scorn yourself
Your destiny is in your hands
It belongs to no one else

Salute my Jamaicans
Who sing all they can
Rasta's sing Black Unity
For the Black Women and Black Man

Salute My Nigerians
In the home of the Black Man
Salute my friends
In the ancient city of Benin

Salute my Zimbabweans
Who fought for liberation
A salute for
a Free Black Nation

A salute for Afroans
Yes, we too, are a nation
One day we all will see
True National Liberation

But first there must be
Much more Black Unity
For sure one Black day
We'll be so free

I salute
All Black Nations
Salutations
To all Black Nations.

Red, Black and Green

I wear Red, Black and Green
When I check out a scene
As an act of pride
Every time I take a ride

One day a sister asked
What is this thing?
Every time you wear
Red, Black and Green

I said Red is for
The bloodshed we have shed
In the past, present and in the future
Our color is Black
And that's a fact

Green is for our land
Home of the Black Man
In our land in Africa
And where we live in America

Wear your Red and Black
Wear Red, Black and Green
With pride walk or ride
Cause it's a serious thing

Wear our Red
And our Black
And our Green
Build up our self-esteem

Wear the colors
Of our nation
And support our drive
For our Liberation

African King/African Queen
Wear Red, Black and Green
Anytime you move
Out on the scene.

Reason

Let's talk together
And reason what it's all about
Any problems we have
We can work them out

Reason together
Turn the matter inside out
Black Family Unite
So we can fight for our rights

Reason about his oppression
Don't put your hand in repression
Don't let them make you a puppet
In a game called Black Oppression

Let the truth come out
Clear up all the doubt
Weigh it carefully
You better check it out

Sit down and reason together
Define that on which we agree
If Black People reason together
We'll discover unity.

African Gin

African Gin
Please my friend
Drink it
Your head will spin

Ogogoro
To quite a few
Never a shortage
Never a queue

Palm wine ferments
Guided by African sense
Ogogoro is clear
And cheaper than beer

Hot enough
To catch a fire
This one sends
The drinker higher

White man said
Illegal
Buy Gordons
How Evil!!!

To Ogogoro of Nigeria
We add herbs
To fight Malaria

Herbs turn it red
Or even pink
This is the time
It's ready to drink

Taste it
I'm telling you
You'll love it
If drinking is what you do

100 or 150 proof
The people's drink
Is quite a brew.

African Palm Wine

It is
Very sweet
As soon as it comes
From the palm tree

Natural
Full of yeast
I love it
Tastes so sweet

African wine
From the tree to me
Natural
I love it sweet

White or brown
Sweet and then sour
That is when
It gains power.

Africa

Hey Blood
I mean
Hey Bro
I mean

Hey Brother Man
Yea, You Black Men
Come on over here
To the Black Man's land
Motherland understand

Drink African wine
Live African life
Eat African Food
Get in the groove

The scheme of things
Is sure to please
If you see an orange
Take a squeeze

Sweet pineapples
Sweet mangos too
Black-eyed peas are local beans
You will see familiar food

Afroans, Africans
Sacrifice
Make your goal
One visit in life.

Africa's Call

Ibo, Edo
Yoruba, Urhobo
Hausa, Etasako
Can you hear?
Africa's call
United We Stand
Divided we fall
Angola, Namibia
Guyana to New Guinea
Open your ears
Africa's call
United we stand
Divided we fall

Cuba, Jamaica
Belize, Bahia
Do you hear?
Africa's Call
United we stand
Divided we fall

Benin, Soweto
Ethiopia, The Congo
Africa, Africans
Those far, those near
Can you hear?
Africa's call
United we stand
Divided we fall.

Let the Love Flow

Brothers and sisters
Hey what's up yo
Yeah Lakeview, Sunnydale,
H.P.B.V. and Fillmore

Let the stupid violence go
Brothers and sisters
Let the love flow

You know we
Are one people
Who have been treated
Every way but equal

If we work together
We have clout
Working together
We can help each other out

If self destruction
Is our path
Fratricide will
Be our wrath
If you know
What we should know
Brothers and sisters
Let the love flow

In Swampy D.
And B.V.H.P.
Army Street
And Alemany

Open your eyes
And you will see
The power we have
With Black Unity

We got to let
the violence go
So we can
Let The Love Flow.

All Across America

All across America
We Blacks have one plight
All Across America
We try to do what is right

All Across America
Police shoot Blacks down
With an all white jury
The guilty are never found

All Across America
We blacks have one sight
That's why we need united brains
For our liberation fight

All Across America
On the other side of the tracks
All Across America
We are the Black

From Black Alabama
To Black Atlanta
From Black New York
To Oakland's Lake Merritt Park

All Across America
We are the Blacks
Since we have one plight
Let's unite for our fight.

Black Roots Black Youth

Black Roots
Soul Truth
Know your history
Black Youth

Black Roots
For real Truth
Keep your ancestry
Black Youth

My apologies
For where we are today
Broken promises
Made things that way

Don't give up
Til the battle is won
If change is to come
You, you are the one

Who says
You must be inferior
Question those
Who claim to be superior

Learn the Black Truth
My Black Youth
And please do not loose
Our Black Roots

Homeless Hotel

They got a hotel
For the Homeless
At the south end
Of the bay

The Homeless Hotel
Of Sunny San Jose

Hotels for the homeless
Homeless Hotels
How can Reagan sell?
The Homeless hotel

After years
Of Star Wars Reagan
All the profits
Are surely taken

We have homeless
Coast to Coast
And hunger hurts
The most

But how can
Reagan sells
The hopeless
Homeless Hotel.

Speak Jazz Please Part 2
Written for African-American History Month 2001

Like a warm
Summer breeze
Like a beautiful
Black woman's squeeze

You can do it hard
Or do it with ease
Horn player don't tease
Speak Jazz Please

Speak and let
Them know
Play Jazz
Low as you can go

Play from the depth
Of our very souls
Like roots, breathe
Through the tall trees

Play Jazz like
Those tall African Trees
Play for our people
Rising from our knees

Play Jazz 3/5ths of a human being
For four hundred years of captivity
And one hundred years
Of trickery where they said
We were free
But we knew, not really

Play for our souls
Play hot let it glow
When you let it go
Play like hot coals

Play so we will grow
Play cause we are to go
For freedom in this century
And attain true liberty

Play Jazz please
Like a warm summer breeze
Play Jazz please
Like a Black Woman's squeeze.

Racial Brothers

Are you Edo
Can you speak Ibo?
Who is Oyibo?
Tell me if you know

Are you a Hausa Man?
Are you a Kanuri Man?
Let us all join together
We are racial brothers

Hey brother man
Are you from yourbaland?
Are you a Shona?
Are you from Zululand?

We Are Racial brothers
Come on Black People let's pull together
Talking to my racial sisters and brothers
Come on Black People let's get it together

I know you been robbed
By some crazy brothers
I've been there too
Why do we harm each other?

Are you a West Indian?
Are you from the Caribbean?
We are blood brothers
We are racial brothers

Blood much thicker than water
And brothers that's a fact
And who needs unity more
Than my fellow Blacks

We are racial brothers
We look like no others
From Black Fathers and Black Mothers
We are racial sisters and brothers.

Love Is Part 2

Love is the simplest
Love is the most complex
Thing in the world
For every man, woman boy and girl
Love is splendid
Love is pain
Love is real
Love is a game
Love is sunlight
Love is rain
Sometimes
Love is a dam shame
A veteran of
One or more of a relationship
I surely know Love is a trip
Look at the sisters
The jazz plays
Just like the
Good old days
You meet a woman
And treat her real nice
She is my sugar
I am her spice
Maybe a day will come
Love is fun
Maybe after awhile
You are on the run
Tons of ladies
In this happy hour tonight
Ladies look good

And the perfume smells right
Look at the girls
Watch their moves
African-American sisters rule
While the brothers drool\par
There is
Love at a glance
Look deeper it maybe a trance
Or a bad chance
Looking for the love
The one that will stick
Love is best I bet your
When love sticks like glue
Love is daylight
Love is night

If you find a real love Maybe, carefully take a bite\par This poem was written at the Phillip R. Bell First Friday Happy Hour at the Spot Light On The Square In Alameda, CA in early May 2001.

People's Love

Where is our people's love
Blessed by God above
When we kill each other
my sister and brother

First love yourself
then love God our maker
then love self and kind
In the killing fields of our communities
Do not be a faker

First love yourself and kind
One love, we must find
Then we could love everyone else
but first we must show a love of self

Once we love ourselves
and stop killing each other
begin anew as a people
to show real love to each brother
and love not mistreat our sister
It will be so easy
to love any other

Find our people's love
In our heart or in God above
One love, my people
then freedom is our sequel.

No More Unjust Wars

No more Korea's
No more Viet Nam's
No more white man's wars
No more El Salvadors

No more being a boy
No more being a white man's toy
No more of their wars
No more El Salvadors

If the army sends you home
I am going to say right on
No more being a tool
No more being a tool

They sent us to the Congo
And to hot spots in the Caribbean
To fight for their kingdom
Here, Black people have no freedom

They sent us to Viet Nam, Mi Lai
To fight for their lie
If you return in a box
Your people are going to cry

First class soldier
Second class citizen
If you are no careful
They'll send you to prison

Better ask yourself if you're afraid?
Cause those generals die in bed
Better ask yourself if it's smart
Better stop that mess before they start
No more unjust wars
No more El Salvadors!!!!!!

Senators and Diplomats

Members of the cabinets
Talking to the president
Senators and Diplomats
Can you feel the cutbacks?

Senators and Diplomats
never feel the cutbacks
If you are in doubt
Ask the Blacks

Budget cutbacks
Cause too many heart attacks
And the safety net
Have far too many cracks

Senators and Diplomats
And the racist president
Who made it by accident
Now he doesn't pay his rent

And when I pay my rent
I don't have one red cent
Unemployment is everywhere
But Ronnie boy doesn't care

Tell me Mister President
Where is your common sense?
How could you feel the cutbacks?
When you hate the Blacks?

And I ask you Blacks
Asking unemployed Blacks?
Do you feel the cutbacks?
Do you feel those cutbacks?

House of Representatives
Where are the incentives?
You mayors get the facts
Police are killing Blacks

Members of the cabinets
Talking to the presidents
Senators and Diplomats
Can you feel those cutbacks?

Afroan Unity

See my people crying
Crying in the street
Living in misery
Because we lack unity

See my people dying
Dealing in the street
No resistance to brutality
Because we lack unity

Afroan Unity conquer Jim Crow
Afroan Unity
Now is the time
Afroan Unity
Our sun must shine

See our people
Walking down the street
See our enemy planning
Police Brutality

See our brother spread eagle
Spread eagle in the street
Racist police only check
A brother's identity

Our sisters oppressed
As you can see
Suffering with dignity
We are fighting to be free

Afroan Unity
Conquer Jim Crow
Afrikan Unity has to grow
Afroan Unity
Now is the time
Afroan Unity
Our sun must shine.

Rise and Win

Although crushed to the earth
We must link up and rise again
Through crushed to American soil
If we unite we'll surely win

Down pressed no progress
Yet we're trying our very best
in oppressing my people
through out the west

And time is the test
Cause we must unify to progress
Analyze what we need
Keep the faith like a mustard seed

Though crushed to this earth
We're not going to join the dirt
Although we're oppressed
We'll unify if we try our very best

Those crushed to the earth
Like truth we'll surely rise again
The crushed sons and daughters of Kush
Must surely rise and win

Over Qualified/It Sho' Is Funky

IT SHO' IS FUNKY
(It sure is funky)
Funk sho' is funky
Funky as a donkey
Funky sho' is funky
It sho' is funky

The party is live from wall to wall
Til daybreak I'm standing tall
I know you will agree with me
It sho' is funy

If you are second-class
Fired first, hired last
Got my degree
No job for me
It sho' is funky

And Brother, if you' in
On a phony rap
A victim in a skin that's Black
No way to be free
In their custody
It sho' is funky

Funk sho' is funky
It's killing you and me
Funky as a donkey
It sho' is funky.

Jim Crow Needs A Beating

Jim Crow
Needs a beating
A people's war
A people's beating

How long
Can Jim Crow madness
Go on
How long will
Afroans silently
Suffer wrong

How long, will they
Shoot us down
What goes
Surely comes around

How long
Discrimination is wrong
How long
Afrocide goes on

How long will
Afroans fear
How long, my brother
Liberation is dear

Raise your hand
Afroan Black Man
A united deathblow
To Jim Crow

Jim Crow is first
Afroans are last
We have to change the
Script and cast

Rise Again

Though crushed
To American earth
We surely must
Rise again

Down but not out
In unity we do have clout
All you have to do
Is check it out

Though crushed
Sons and Daughters of Kush
We must surely
Rise again and again
Until Black Liberation is won

3-39-01   9:45pm

Black California

Listen to voices of the oppressed
Listen to hear voices protest
At the bottom of the heap
The feelings run very deep

California, leading the nation?
Well-oppressed Blacks seek Liberation
Racists patrol the Black Community
And police shoot with immunity

Black California is not free
Held at San Quentin-jailed at Tracy
The bars are contracted in our mind
Cause being Black is a crime

Black California from L.A.
To Frisco, the city by the bay
I heard a brother from Fresno say
Free my people, this very day

It's A Black Thang: You Could Not Understand

Like eating the left overs
After working the fields
And wept on our backs
Because of lower yields

Convicted in
A skin that's Black
And all of your people
Are under attack

No, you cannot understand
What it is to be a Black
Women or a Black Man

Forced to eat pig guts, knuckles,
Hoofs, heads and tails
Forced in to slavery
Poverty and jails

It is the truth
More than slang
You better to know
It's a black thang

As long as our
African American nation
Lives with in our hearts
No government can
Ban it or destroy it

You see
It's a black thang
You could not understand.

A Poem for Dr. Jocob Crawford

A good brother
Not up in age
With a cool head
Is now dead

He was my dentist
He was my friend
An OMI-Pilgrim board member
But always a good friend

A graduate of USF
And other varsities too
A very good person
Who did not make the news?

Always a smile
On his face
A sensitive dentist
A credit to our race

Providing quality dental services
To his clientele
I know God will
Greet you well

So long my brother!

My Dream

My dream is for Black Kings
My dream is for Black Queens
My dream is to unify the Black Nation
My dream is for Black Liberation

The order is given for an attack
Divided we cannot do anything
United we can drive them back

We are despised in this land
Unite Black minds I know we can
Come on Black woman
Come on Black Man

The healing power of love
Is what we are made of?
Keep it warm not cold
Let it flow from our inner soul

My dream is for beautiful black cream
My dream is for beautiful Black queens
For strong black kings
For pretty black genes
MY DREAM, MY DREAM, MY DREAM.

Red, Black and Green II

The Red, Black and Green
Is a real serious thing
Meant to uplift and unite
The African King and Queen

Wear Red, Black and Green
To chill out the gang war thing
Wear Red, Black and Green
Don't be so mean

Wear Red, Black and Green
Join Black people's team
Wear Red, Black and Green
African King/African Queen

Stop calling each other niggers
Or bitches or hoes
Because we are family
Kin and friends not foes

Stop calling your brother nigger
Get your hand off that trigger
We got to stop being fools
And own gravedigger

Red, Black and Green
Is a serious thing
Meant to uplift and unite
The African King and Queen.

Celebrating Our Culture

Celebrate our being
Celebrate our culture
Celebrate our soul
Celebrate our role

Celebrate our land
Where we come from
Celebrate our Africa
Africans in America

Understand what existed
Before the white man
Understand our history
In our Black Ancestral land

Self Respect atop the tree
Love our tree of life
Self-love builds self-esteem
For African Kings and Queens

Nurture our spirit of life
Inside our concrete Jungle
Use our common sense
Celebrate our African essence

Value black life/culture
Learn failure/successes
In our very own history
Motivate yourself for victory

Foster homogenius unity
Rise above the misery
Of rejection of today and slavery
Network to Liberation, be free

Lift up bowed heads
Stop our assistance of genocide
Rise up red, black and green
Rise up black King/Black Queen

Release yourself from hopelessness
From inside your limitless mind
Inspiration for black liberation
Is the strength you find?

Discover the essence of our kind
Please develop your/our mind
Appreciate what we are
We must be our own star

And that is what you are
And that is what we are
We must be our own star

Beautiful African Kings and Queens
In America from Africa afar.

Off Your Backs

Off your Backs
All you Blacks
Off your knees please

Over come 400 years
Of fears and tears
Pick up your spears

Think about disunity
In our community
Surely unity is the key

Like five fingers
We must unite
Black unity is dynamite

Off your knees please
Off your backs
I'm talking to
All you Blacks.

Frisco Blues

So Sad
The headline said
Two wounded
One killed dead

It was Lakeview
Could be Bayview
It was in the news
Call it Frisco Blues

Youth gone turf crazy
They don't treat a sister like a lady
The oppressed paying dues
Cause we in Frisco Blues

Down in Sunnydale
Up on the hill
Why on earth
Must black blood spill

East coast or west
Wake up the rest
Make Black unity the news
Or continue Frisco Blues

Look at all them bad dudes
Where's the brains in their shoes
From Brooklyn L.A. to New Port News
You can hear us cry Frisco Blues

From one brother to another
One brother to sisters
From one community
to the other

To every black man
On American land
To every black woman
To every African American

To our Black youth
Try to seek the truth
Develop a plan
And please understand

Divided we fall
United we stand
Divided we fall
United we stand

Dedicated to Johnnie Hodge's and 25 other African American youth killed in the last 2 years in San Francisco and the surviving victims and families.

Who Are the Afroans

Millions of Africans
Taken away
Millions lost
And bred in slavery

Millions of soul brothers
And soul sisters too
Made to carry the shame
Of no national or tribal name

To call us a Negro is but a joke
To call us Black Amerikkkan
Exhibits the colonial yoke

Africans born in America
That is what we are
Though located in Amerikkka
Africa is our origin and star

Millions of Afroans
Fighting for liberation
Millions of Africans
The African-American nation.

Another Brother Has Been Shot

It was a sunny California day
We were taking a ride to L.A.
The sun was shinning, hiding decay
Black folks hoping for a better day

Talking to a good brother man
About one Sister Love killed by a policeman
That was 1979 understand
No mercy for a Black Man

Well the city of angels is very hot
Another brother has been shot
This is 1980 understand
No mercy for the Black Man

Nothing worst than a racist cop
A weak Black mayor is a total flop
Well the city of angels is very hot
Another brother has been shot.

It Couldn't be Done
(Run Jessie Run)

They said
It couldn't be done
They said
You'll never be No. 1
They said
It couldn't be done
Run Jessie Run

They said you'd spoil it
For #1
They said your battle
Would never be won
They said
It couldn't be done
Run Jessie Run

They said
You'd never be #1
But you are
Our favorite son chorus
They said
It couldn't be done
Run Jessie Run

They said
It couldn't be done
Run Jessie Run
They said
It couldn't be done
Run Jessie Run
Run till the battle is won

Jessie Jackson ran for President in 1984 and 1988

History of Our Struggle

History of Black Struggle
Is a story
About a lot of trouble
In our History

After building pyramids
And creating geometry
We captured
And kidnapped into slavery

Where we survived
The middle passage
And lived down
Their genocidal carnage

Producing Martin R. Dalaney
And Toussiant Le overture
And Nat Turner
Our freedom was matured

Oppressed for generations
Western Hemisphere black nations
The history of our struggle
Is history of a lot of trouble

Cause we don't live
In a bubble
Could not walk
We had to run double

Receiving their scorn
Feeling their harm
We lost self-love
In a slavery storm

We produced Marcus Garvey
To open our eye
To give us Red, Black and Green
To the Black King and Queen

We produced Elijah Muhammad
To do for self
He taught us to
Defend on no one else

We produced Malcolm and Martin
To unite our dream
Advancing toward liberation
Here me black nation

And we must go on
So we can get strong
Cause the History
Of Black Struggle
Is beautiful survival
In Babylon's trouble.

Healing

Got all of them cuts
On your head
More bullets fly
My brother is dead

So we got to
Stop the killing
Brothers work it out
Start the healing

In the hood
On the block
In our community
Around the clock

Don't raise your hand
Against a brother
Don't raise that gun
Let us get it together

You know
How your mother's feeling
about all this
Brother to brother killing

If you love our people
Let it show
If we unite
We'll progress and grow

Don't do it to yourself
Or no one else
In the hood
Is it understood

United
We got a chance
Divided
We can't dance

Stop killing each other
In the neighborhood
We need more
Sister and brotherhood

Don't just be
Reeling
From the Bullets
You're feeling
Stop the killing
Start the healing.

If We Could?

If we could
Love each other
Like sister
And brother

We wouldn't be
Looked at as a fool by others
We would be
United sisters and brothers

We would be
Working together
In unity my sister
And brother

If only we
Could love each other
My people
Like sister and brother

We could build
Another pyramid
You know that
Is what we did

We could work
For our freedom together
Progress my sister
Rise up my brother

We could unite
Our community
We could unite
Our family

If only we could
Love each other
Then we would
Really have it together.

Fighting in the Streets
(Dedicated to Nigerian Taxi Drivers)

When you see Black People
Fighting in the Street
When the blood starts flowing
It's not so sweet

Black Folks fighting
Each other in the Street
When we need to fight
So the Black Race can be free

Some are fighting
No money for rent
Some are fighting
To be the President

Some are fighting
For a car accident
Killing each other
Because of a small dent

Few are fighting
Our real enemy
Too few are fighting
So the Black Race can be free

Stop brothers and sisters
This fighting in the street
When the blood starts flowing
It's killing you and me.

I'm Proud

Say it loud
I'm Black and
I'm Proud

Say it loud
I'm Black and
I'm proud

James Brown
Wrote this song
In the sixties
When we were strong

Say it loud
I'm Black and
I'm proud

James Brown
Once sang this song
But I need you
for this poem

Say it loud
I'm Black and
I'm Proud

We work hard
We are Black
The original people
And that's a fact

Up from segregation
We want
Black Liberation

Say it loud
I'm Black and
I'm Proud

Say it loud
I'm Black and
I'm Proud.

Black on Black Crime

Tis the shame of our time
Black man's sun don't shine
It can blow your mind
Talking about Black on Black Crime

It happens to you and me
Things unprogressive brothers do
My people it's not so sweet
Black on Black crime in the street

It could be Lagos
It could be Frisco
It could be Kingston
Or Roxbury Boston

KKK accomplishes
The reverse racists
Tis the shame of our time
Black on Black crime.

We Are Together

African Man
My Brother, My Friend
African Woman
My Sister, My Kin

One aim, one destiny
We struggle in unity

African people
We are together
Brothers and Sisters
United forever

Down with exploitation
of our life and soul
We stand together
The young and the old

Down with our foes
Apartheid and Jim Crow
Down with colonial mentality
And that of the Negro

Scattered we stand
On many a land
The Black Woman
The Black Man

African people
We are together
Brothers and Sisters
United forever.

Lagos Remembered

Lagos Remembered

It's a Capital City
It's ugly and pretty
Just no pity
Like a New York City

Full of Historic places
And walls of Black faces
With black soldiers and black police
And beer by the cases

There is Oba's palace
And pretty sunshine
And many of the sisters
Are very fine

Check out Bar Beach
And many lagoons
While the air is filled
With Reggae tunes

Watch out for the Ben
While you are making friends
Observe how the Nigerians
Deal with Western trends

From Ikeja to Ikoui
Truly a colorful story
And there are a few ghettos
One will see

While the customs
Of our past are preserved
So they will last.

This Is Your Ancestors

In Mother Afrika
We sat safely
In the center
of the world

For years and years and years
Then they came
Money missionaries marines
Causing tears, death and fears

A lot of us
Were taken
Captivity
Some died silently
Some fought to be free

Don't act
Like you don't know
What to do
This is your Ancestors
Talking to you.

African People Are Beautiful

African people have pretty eyes
African women have pretty thighs
African people have pretty lips
African women have pretty hips

African people on many trips
African people came on slave ships
African people dark to fair
African people have pretty hair

African people have a pretty nose
African people make pretty clothes
African people will never fade
Not the African people GOD made

African people have a developed mind
African people can be so kind
African people have pretty Black skin
African people we are all kin

African unity is wonderful
African unity is powerful
African people be truthful
Because African people are beautiful.

Beauty is Soul Deep
Written 2/11/83

Broken glass in the street
Broken dreams on their feet
Beauty is a surface sheet
Beauty is soul deep.

Among broken hopes and dreams
One can find beauty it seams
One thing don't be no sheep
Taking orders from a creep.

Do we hate each other?
Or do we love each other?
Life can be better
My sister, my brother

The beauty of a Black sister
And the beauty of a brother
From the natural hair to their feet
Beauty is soul deep.

Life is Love

Life is love
Love is life
Life is no show
Everyone should know

Love is life
Life is love
Know all elements
Life is made of

Life is love
Love is life
Southern Africa
Amerikkka
Torn by racial strife

Life is live
When sweet and long
If we close our eyes
Afrocide goes on

Ignoring Black People's struggle
Soul musicians are wrong
Singing only the love song

If you got to be commercial
There is something you should know
Afroan people want Freedom
Not Jim Crow

Soul Brothers and Sisters
Lend me your ears
Brothers and Sisters
Come near and hear

Love is Life
Life is love
Know all elements
What life is made of?

Tribute to Our Family

I remember
Trips by car
To Los Angeles
And our Dad buying
All Seven of us hamburgers
NEVER A HUNGRY DAY

I remember
Taking a bath in a bucket
In the shower of the
Old projects in 1960
At South Ridge Road and La Salle
Hunters Point San Francisco
And playing with Jerome Fell

I remember
Moving to Lakeview in 1961
We were happy to move
Into a house at 38 Brighton Avenue
And jumping from
A table red
And landing on
Our strong steel framed bed

This is a tribute
To my family
Live on in unity
We are colorful
And many shades of Black

And true diversity
Rooted in love
True respect
United in our destiny

Can our Mom's
Tender care
Cease towards the
Child she bears

In our family
Mom's love will
Always be there
And our late Daddy Redd
We all remember
What he said
Family comes first
Through the best
And through the worst

When Dad died
We united and cried
What a tragedy
For our family
But Dad had to transcend
And go on to heaven

While we continued
To love GOD and life
And our family
And we survived!!!!

Black Peace and Black Power

Stand up and holler
Black Peace and Black Power
Stand up and holler
Black Peace and Black Power

Let Black Peace Reign
Unity is the key to the game
Let Black Peace reign
Black on Black crime is the shame

Black Peace in the Ghetto
And throughout the Black Community
Black Peace in the Ghetto
Black Peace in the Black Family

Black Peace on Black turf
Black Peace cause it too rough
Black Peace out there on the streets
Brothers and Sisters Black Peace Please

Stand up and holler
Black Peace and Black Power
Stand up and holler
Black Peace and then Black Power.

We Gone Be Free
(We Are Going to be Free)

When we start sharing
A Love Supreme
A for real love supreme
And stop killing each other

When we start to educate
Feed, clothe, house, organize
And define ourselves
When we start to unite our people
We gonna be free

When powerful Black minds
In beautiful Black bodies
Frame a Black Nation
When I unite with you and you unite with me
When I unite with you and you unite with me
That is when we all will be free.

The Chains Are On Our Mind

We no longer have chains
On our hands and feet
They are on our mind

The thorough brainwashing
We received
Made us blind

We copy everyone
In this world
Yet despise ourselves

To say we are Black today is a fact
Because of brainwashing
Some deny being Africans

Yes, we've been brainwashed
For a long, long time
The chains of slavery have been changed

From our hands and feet
And slipped on our mind.

Thousands of Afroans

Thousands of Afroans
Needed for a war
We have to kill
Jim Crow

Millions of Afrikans
That's what we are
All are needed
To fight the war

Jim Crow Apartheid
Afroans take aim
Sound our guns
This ain't no game

Thousands of Afroans
Vanguard of the millions
War against racism
War against Jim Crow Against
Afrocide and oppression
We all feel and know.

Reaganomic Blues

Got us singing
Economic blues
And who are they
Reagan and his fools

Some people die
Or live on the street
Or in their cars
Or on their feet

The Reagan Economy
Regan I hate your policy
As the rich get richer
And the poor get poorer

My people paying dues
Just because Reagan rules
We all got
Reaganomic Blues.

I Salute Marvin Gaye

The need
Has never been greater
For more Black Unity
In our Black Community

The need is there
Can you open your mind?
Check out the atrocity
That you will find

Must a father
Shoot his own son
Before we realize
Black Unity is Priority #1

When Marvin Asked
What's going on?
We all shouted
Brother, Right on

And now we find
Marvin Gaye is gone
And again we ask
What's going on?

Let Blacks join hands
Let us rejoin our hearts
For more Black Unity
In our Black Community

Raise the level
Of Black Affinity
Rekindle kindred spirits
Renew self-love for Black Unity

Reduce the running of games
Reduce the need for shame
Reduce our suicidal drift
Black Unity is our aim

The need
Has never been Greater
For more, more Black Unity
In our Black community

Written at 3:00 AM 4-6-84
And dedicated to the living Spirit of Marvin Gaye.

Black Woman, You are a Poem

I saw you on United Airlines
I saw you homeless in San Francisco
Another time in Chicago, you said
Your red black and green is live not dead

Most appreciated Black Woman
Though disrespected by some
To me my sister
You are number 1

We are nothing without you
We are whole with you
Cause you can be real
And that we can feel

You are our rhythm and soul
You are our rhyme
You are our future's producer
Making history and the future in our time

You are our beauty and
You are our survival
Please don't leave a Black man
For any other rival

Cause you are our soul
Our future continuation
Mother of our Black Nation
Work with us for liberation

And you are our compliment
Reflect us like the moon
Stick by us
And we will obtain our liberation soon

Because though are
Not quite what we should be
Held back and oppressed by white society
You and I are, one entity

Black woman you are a poem
You black history in motion
We really love you
With all of our real devotion

And though we are not free
Or all we want to be
We cherish your company
And love and appreciate you totally.

Brothers Killing Brothers

Brothers massacring brothers
Brothers being massacred by others
When will it all end
When will we be friends?

Brothers assassinating brothers
Brothers being assassinated by others
When will it all end
And treat each other as a friend.

Brothers killing brothers
Brothers being killed by others
When will all turf end
Can we treat each other like a friend?

What happened to live and let live
Why is it death we give?
Pumping bullets into each other's head
Too many young brothers are dead

Brothers beating sisters
Brothers beating down brothers
Brothers being beat by others
How can we go any further????

Brothers killing brothers
Brothers being killed by others
Can we have a truce?
And stop the killing of our brothers.

Identity to Those Ashamed of our Name

400 Years Ago
Is when we came?
And African
Was our name?

Africa is rich
Gold was/is her fame
400 years ago
Our ancestors came

In Africa we have
4 million years
Of Africa Culture
History and Fame

How could we
Those kissed by the sun
Give up
Before the battle is won

How could we be ashamed?
Of our history and fame
How could we be ashamed
Of our very own name

Written for Black History Month 1984

Stop Police Brutality

Dedicated to all Victims of Police/Prison Guard Brutality

Stop Police Brutality
You violate democracy
Using it mostly against the Blacks
You practice treason and hypocracy

Stop this insanity
Or is this white vanity
One truth is for sure
It's a crime against humanity

Stop Police Brutality
The often-deadly reality
If this is democracy
Stop this atrocity

You got itchy trigger fingers
And you know what it engenders
Bad Police Community Relations
Cause Police oppressed the Black Nation

You are easily excitable
On the take for action
At the drop of a hat
You're ready for batter a Black

Don't think you will get away
Cause one day you will surely pay
It's unjustifiable homicide
To black folks its pure genocide

Stop Police Brutality
Innocent until proven guilty
Don't be judge, jury and executioner
Stop this crime against humanity

White police brutality
In the Black Community
Stop this white insanity
Stop Police brutality.

Raid on the Treasury

Reagan and his cronies
Are raiding the U.S. till
625 Million R&D
For MX Missiles
No money for
A liver transplant
For the elderly
On Social Security
And how do you feel
When right in your face
Your are going to witness
A billion dollar waste
A billion dollar waste
Regan and the defense industry
Goanna do it to the treasury
And the House of Representatives
Really have no substance
Giving the people cheese
Can you feel the Reaganonics freeze?
One billion for the thieves
20 million unemployed
Vote with your feet
Or be destroyed
They are plundering
The national treasury
The deficit business
Is for you and me
So they can blow up
The world and the whole dam sky

Blow the world asunder
With Nuclear Thunder
Better Dead
Than Peace with the Red
D.O.D.
Is in the dead
Slice up the pie
While the poor don't eat.

Spontaneous January 1984

Thoughs abound
For the liberation not found
As we enter 84
And Reagan says invade some more

Thoughts for the tax
I must plan to pay
So Ronald Reagan
Can do it his way

And the jobs
My people need
And the Black Nation
We got to feed

We have to defeat
Those who hold our neck with their feet
An Anti Black system
Offers Black Freedom.

Extermination

If you ignore
Our liberation
We all face
Extermination
Or Domination
Close your eyes
Like you don't see
We Blacks need
More Unity
The flow of Black Blood
The lack of self-love
And white supremacy
An implacable enemy
If you ignore
Black Liberation
We all face
White domination.

Freedom, Freedom, Freedom

We want to write a freed song
We want our people to say right on
Please help me sing a freedom song
Freedom, Freedom, Freedom

We need to write a freedom song
If we unite, we will be so strong
We need to sing a freedom song
Freedom, Freedom, Freedom

Africa needs a freedom song
We all know Apartheid is so wrong
That's why we sing a freedom song
Freedom, Freedom, Freedom

We need a freedom song
We have been held down too long
Please help us sing a Freedom song
Freedom, Freedom, Freedom

We want to write a Freedom song
Our people have been oppressed too long
Oppression of the Black is wrong
Freedom, Freedom, Freedom

Can you hear the Freedom song?
Black Folks stand up and say right on
We're writing so we can be strong
Freedom, Freedom, Freedom.

Class 5 A Unity Rap

We need unity
We need harmony
We need unity
We need harmony

We need unity
We need Harmony
In on our classroom
Today is not too soon

Unity is needed
By you and me
Harmony is better
Can't you see?

We can learn more
With harmony
Open up the door
With unity

Can we all
Sing a song
Can we all
Get along

Dedicated to all Bret Harte Elementary School Students

Intimidation

Don't lie down intimidation
Don't submit
A liberation resignation

They are only bluffing
With tactics of intimidation
Have no fear
Rise up my Black Nation

Don't succumb
Don't concede
Don't give up
On what we really need

They will tell you
"You haven't got a chance"
In the name of Black Liberation
We must advance

They will tell you
"Don't make waves"
That is what they told
The slaves in unmarked graves

They will tell you
"You really need me boy"
But true Black liberation
Will bring about Black joy

They will tell you
"Be happy with what you got"
They will tell you
"Don't let things get too hot"

But don't the swayed
By what they do and say
As we establish liberation
We established a brand new day.

Written in 1968 or 1969 (Original Version)

For You And Me

Let your mind
Body
Heart
and Soul
Run Wild

With African feelings
Be shaken
With an inspiration
Generating
African vibrating
Action making
Liberation taking
African love for
The African Race.

I Saw Them

I saw them
Those Black Leaders
Those Black Liberation
Soldiers and generals

Marching with dignity
Marching in harmony
Marching together
For African American unity

It was the
Million Man March
Caring freedom's torch
Millions of African-Americans
Men, women, boys and girls

Proud men with their sons
Even proud sisters
With their daughters
Marching in unity toward our new destiny

I saw Marcus, Muhammad, and Martin
Stokely and Malcolm
I saw Bethune,
Harriet, and Nat Turner

I saw Farrakhan,
Jackson and Sharpton
I saw Congress Lady Brenda Lee
And Congress Lady Maxine Waters

I saw them all
Marching in unity
I saw them all
Marching to our new destiny.

Who Are We?

Who are we?
Who are we?
Are we Negroes?
Are we Negroes?

No! No! No! No!
We are African people
We are African people

Brother can't you hear?
Sister can't you hear?
We are African people
We are African people

Who are we?
Who are we?
Are we colored people?
Are we colored people?

No! No! No! No!
We are African people!
We are African people!

Who are we?
Who are we?
Are we N's?
Are we N's?

No! No! No! No!
We are African people!
We are African people!

Brother can't you hear?
Sister can't you hear?
We are African people!
We are African people!

In Sweet Benin

On the scene
In sweet Benin
You can see
Almost anything

On the scene
In sweet Benin
See the people
Doing their thing

In the market
The women sell and buy
In the bars
Some men drink

In the offices
Some people are cheating
But you better know
The people are seeing
And seeing is believing

On the scene
In sweet Benin
The Black Man is King
And Black Woman is Queen

And live is the night scene
The people dance and the people sing
Disco houses throughout Benin
Come on baby let's do our thing

On the streets of Benin
Eat barbecue called suya
See our culture sing
Check out the scene in Sweet Benin.

A Day in June

Green is the grass, the day overcast
The rainy season is here at last
Gallops become mini ponds
Rain some more, let the food grow

Farmers are happy
The weather is cool
Roasted corn on the cob
The end of school

Sunshine sneaks in
Kissing the motorists and pedestrians
Ikebes are moving, tempting good men

The girls are back from far off schools
The town is 'live, watch their moves
Sunshine is broken by a tropical rain
While traders hustle for their tarpaulin.

Benin Arrival

It was a rainy
Tropical African night
We made Benin
On the last evening flight

Something on
A golf tournament
Hotel rooms commandeered
By the Government

This was my arrival
in Bendal
We spent the first night
At Central Hotel.

Expression

Poetic Expression
Has more protection
Than a Black Person
Many times on American land

A dog or cat
Can get more respect
Than a black woman
Like Tawana Brawley can expect

That's the facts
Feelings expressed by many black
As a foot stands on our neck
We're held down like rats

Huh! American Democracy
No, It's hypocrisy
Land of the free
No, the land of old/new slavery.

All Across America

We Blacks have one plight
All Across America
We try to do what is right

All Across America
Police shoot Blacks down
With an all white jury
The guilty are never found

All Across America
We blacks have one sight
That's why we need united brains
For our liberation fight

All Across America
On the other side of the tracks
All Across America
We are the Black

From Black Alabama
To Black Atlanta
From Black New York
To Oakland's Lake Merritt Park

All Across America
We are the Blacks
Since we have one plight
Let's unite for our fight.

Tree of Life

Part 1

You are
The tree of life
You are
The source of spice

You are
The carrier of our black seed
You are
All we really need

You are
The source of our civilization
You are
The mother of our Black Nation

The world is rough
And full of strife
But you, you are
Our precious tree of life

Part 2

Black Women
Is my tree of life?
My mothers and sisters
My aunts and aunties

Black Women
Tree of life
You're the lovers
Of me and my brothers

Stand by us
In this white supremacy world
Though we may not say enough
We need you Black Women/girl

On African Land

On African Land
On green foliage hills
and fertile plateaus
and dusty dirt roads

And the cultural setting
Of the old and new
Cross a river in a canoe
With an African crew

From the tropical south
To the flat plains
of Nigeria's north
View Benin's art

And those tall African trees
And a people off their knees
Life in a black country
Is really something to see

You can arrive by air
And see a taxi there
A taste of life
With all the spice

The Black woman is queen
On the African screen
Home of the Black Man
On African LAND.

Chimarenga

Chimarenga
War of Liberation
Rise up you
Mighty black nation

Chimarenga
Is for the degradation
Chimarenga
End of the humiliation

War with the pen
War with the words
War with the arms
But go to
War with self-love

Chimarenga
Against discrimination
Chimarenga
Against domination

War of Liberation
War with education
War with Black Awareness
War of my Black Nation

Become Yourself

Black woman, Black woman
Take off your white mask
Become yourself at last

Take the white chains
Off your mind
Cleanse your body and soul
Of the white dreams
We all hold

Deal with Black realities

Black Man, Black Woman
The whiteness in all of our minds
Has kept us divided too long of a time
Try, Try, Try

To be our natural African selves
Not someone else
Then the white madness
In our African mind

Will become smaller in time
In Black societies
Deal with the Black realities!

Dedicated to Young African-Americans

Young Blacks
In America
Do you know?
We come from Africa

Do you know?
How we got here
Do you think?
There's nothing to fear

When it's dog bites
Or hanging like kites
Put your sights
On fighting for your rights

Check out the wisdom
Of the ages
Our history and Tradition
Our current situation

To be young gifted
And Black
Is where it's at
If you are young and black.

Jet Ride With a Sister

She has soft looking
Beautiful Black skin
The kind you look at
And wish you were touching

Wrapped in braided hair
The white boys dare to stare
Exotic Black
You want to attract

She sits there
Listening to her CD
We talk a little
She is spoken for, not for me.

A Luta Continua

We fight
For what we know is right
A Luta Continua
The struggle continues

From the Congo
To Soweto
From JoBurg to Pittsburg
A Luta Continua

On the Islands
On the Mainland
In the bush
On the secret
The struggle continues

From San Jose's Williams Street Park
To New York
From the Caribbean
To the continent
A Luta Continua

From North Richmond
To the west bay
Lagos, Maputo to Zimbabwe

For Independence
and Liberation
An end to oppression
Of the International African Nation
The struggle continues.

Benin Arrival

It was a rainy
Tropical African night
We made Benin
On the last evening flight

Something on
A golf tournament
Hotel rooms commandeered
By the Government

This was my arrival
In Bendal
We spent the first night
At Central Hotel.

Journey to the Motherland

By an African-American
A journey by air
A journey to share

Journey if you dare
Follow me and go there
Journey to our motherland
By a San Francisco born Black Man

This part is a true story
To see what my land would show me
About a San Francisco homie
Some of you know me

My journey to Nigeria
By way of Liberia
North, South, East and West
I liked the Midwest best

My journey started in Lagos
Traveled North to Kaduna/Zaria/Kano
Traveled South to Benin and Port H
Then the East always promoting peace

Journey to my land
Journey to feel and understand
Journey to our ancestor's land
Journey to our Motherland.

Calling on Our Ancestors

Calling on our ancestors
For a spiritual hand
For Africans in our mother land

Call those who came before
Come back again
Stand nearby and protect us
In a Babylon full of sin

Calling African spirits
From every land
Stand with us
African Woman/African man

Calling on our ancestors
And Jah for a spiritual hand
""For Africans in the Diaspora
And Africans in our Mother Land.

African Moon

I have sat under the African sun
My body soaking wet from its heat
We Blacks sit under the African sun
With tempered skins, no sunburn

I have sat under the African moon
Counting the stars
Thinking of my people's forced journey afar
Where some don't know who they are

I have sat under the African moon
On African dirt, my land
From one end of the right
Until the coming of a morning sunlight

I have sat thinking
I have sat feeling
The power of being Black
Wondering where is our power to act

I have sat under Africa's moon
Hoping liberation would come soon
Hoping for the liberation of my people
Sitting under my African moon.

Airport in Benin

At the African airport
In old sweet Benin
See the women
In their prettiest things

The wrappers and the dresses
The Mrs. and the Misses
In ole Sweet Benin
See the passengers, relative
And friends
But only the passengers are flying

50 dobo parking fee
Or trek in on your feet
The jet will land and turn around
Before the flight out of town

Then there is a short bus ride
Load up and the take off stride
Just to leave sweet Benin
The women wear their pretty things.

Happy Kwanzaa 83-84

Go to see
Activist friends
To reunite
Once again

To make 84
A year of Black affinity
To make 84
A year of Black unity

A Affinity for our brothers
Affinity for our sisters
Affinity for our people
Affinity my people

Affinity for unity
Affinity for our mind
Affinity for Black sanity
Affinity for our kind.

We Are the Unsung Heroes

We are the unsung heroes
What we have suffered
No one knows
And where it will stop
No one knows

Unsung brothers beating odds
And when the police kill us
That's how it goes
And that is how it goes
For us unsung heroes

This system swallows our youth
And our youth don't see the truth
And while they build more jails
Our youth's attempt to steal fails
In a world of craziness

You got to have common sense
And that's how it goes
For the unsung heroes
For this liberation war
We must defeat our foes

To us, the unsung heroes
We fight for our liberation
We fight against foes
Who seek permanent domination?

We can see what it is
Because Uncle Sam is ultimately his
And we are hanging on
Hoping that we will get strong
In our unity we find our strength

We are right they are wrong
This is the unsung song
And that's how it goes
For us, the unsung heroes.

Writing For Eternity

First I write for me
Then I write for "We"
Who survived the middle passage?
I write for eternity

Media recognition
is for the white author
Popular acclaim
You know money and fame

I am a serious writer
I am a freedom fighter
In an era of uncertainty
I am writing for eternity

Not going to write about chestnuts
I am not a commercial quantity
Writing for posterity
Writing for eternity.

Feeling Good in Africa

Family we are forever
We survive any weather
In our people's land
Home of the Black Man

My friend Pat Finn
Bought the drink
I am free
I can think

I'm feeling good in Africa
So good in Africa
In Black Africa
My people's Africa

Where sisters do what is good
And brothers carve from black wood
Here we are in Africa
Black People's Africa

Where a Black Government
Is the master of development
Many she-goats and rams
And afternoon traffic jams

Don't ask for me
In ole Frisco
If you're cool
You will know

I'm feeling good in Africa
So good in Africa
In Black Africa
My people's Africa.

As I am

Accept me as I am
And I'll always be near
Accept me not
And I'm out of here, my dear

Accept me as I am
Or lose our relationship
Just as I am
Or I'll split

So much of each other
We can enjoy
Better be real
Don't be coy

We are different
We are not the same
To lose this love
Will be a shame

But if you try to
Make love a game
We'll split
And you will bear the blame.

The Irony of it All

The irony of it all,
you rise and you fall
The Blacks were standing tall
Until our downfall

In Egypt, Zimbabwe
In the Congo and Songhay
In the Black mainstream
Do you know what I mean?

Whether we are short
Or very very tall
The irony of it all
You rise and you fall

America, South Africa
Caribbean and Pacifica
White feet stampede
On Black hopes and dreams

The scars are deep
What's yours you keep?
It's white domination
Versus Black Liberation

The irony of it all
In Zimbabwe and Songhay
Black Men stood tall

In Egypt and the Congo
Black Women stood tall
Until a historical decline and fall
That is the irony of it all

Blacks all over the world
Some take orders from whites
Blacks all over the world
Fighting for our rights

The Black Race Ruled our destiny
Until our down fall
The irony of it all
You rise and you fall

United We Stand—Divided We Fall.

Love Your Flavor

I like your flavor
It's your savor
To the last drop
Love you, can't stop

Love your flavor
When it is cold
Love your flavor
When it is hot

Love you when
We are together
Love you when
We are apart

Love you when
When you do me a favor
Let me love you
And enjoy your flavor.

God Give Um Freedom

The evil plots
Must surely stop
Shooting wild shots
Must surely stop

Or must God
Come back to this life
Before we end
Senseless violence and strife

Give justice
To the people
If they are occupied
Give um freedom

To the sick
God give um healing
To the insensitive
God give um feeling

To the selfish
Give them a blessing
To know the joy
Of giving and sharing

And to the refugees and oppressed
God give um power
To overcome oppressors
God give um freedom.

Continuously

Loving you
In the morning
That is just
How it is

Loving you in
The afternoon
Hoping to
See you soon

Loving you
Day and night
Loving you
And knowing it is right

Continuously
You and me
Continuously
In love you see.

Peace to the Motherland

No more tribal war
Every one is a star
Peace to the Blackman
Peace to our motherland

Stop persecution
Stop all oppression
Stop military occupation
Let's bring to life, liberation

Peace to every land
Peace to the Brown Man of Palestine
Liberation for all
Peace to every woman

Let every vote count
Let's take a progressive stand
Peace to the African-Americans
Peace to our motherland

Give us justice
Give us peace
Peace to the Black Woman
PEACE TO OUR MOTHERLAND.

There is a Poem

There is a poem
up in me
Expressed
in my poetry

Like unilateralism
white folks go it alone
will poor Black soldiers
die attacking Blacks in Iraq

Will the poor man die?
to make an oil man rich?
what a cost
in human life
In another unjust war
To control the oil for the American car

We remember the pole tax
and Anti Black white attacks
we remember slavery
and still we experience police brutality
and racial discrimination
stereotyping, racial profiling
and the Sheriff's roadblock
near a Florida polling station
is this really liberation?

There is poetry up in me
expressed in my poetry.

Whence We Came

Together we are hundreds
Of millions strong
If we are divided
Discrimination, colonialism and slavery go on

United we are hundreds
Of millions strong
Separated we may not
last too long

African-Americans
From whence we came
Africa is the root
Of our name

From whence we came
African is our name
Be proud!! No shame
Africa is our roots and fame

I heard a brother say
I no be African
I heard a sister say
I am not African

Black brothers and sisters
All over the world
One people, every man
Woman, boy and girl.

Words of Inspiration

Step up to the plate
Please don't fake
There is Progress
We have to make

Joe Clark had a bat
All we have is software and a poem
if you graduate before June
we'll sing a happy song

Work hard everyday
stay on task
to make graduation your focus
and time will go by fast

Don't hate, don't fake
and don't hesitate
focus on your high school diploma
Don't hate, graduate

*Dedicated to past, present and future graduates of the GPA,
OnTI Charles Minor coined the phase Don't Hate, Graduate.*

Free Palestine

Blood running
like water
In the holy land
There is a holocaust
killing off the Palestinians
54 years of
a lopsided pro-Israel policy
but it's the Parisians
Suffering a catrosphy
American bombs
falling from American jets
American helicopters
and American tanks
on ancient Palestine
and it's time
to see a free
Palestine
Stop this new genocide
by Israeli nazi Sharon
so Palestine can be free

Stop bombing
the refugee camps
So Palestine can
print their own stamps

Written 4/20/02 at 10:20am

When it All

When it all
Comes together
We will all
love each other

Treat each sister
Or Brother
Better than
any other

When it all comes together
We will be birds of the same feather
We will then be heavy
And light as a feather

Because whatever the weather
We will be rising up together

Instead of beating each other
As a people
Ready for the next stage
When it all comes together
We'll all love each other.

The Faces of Africa

There are many faces
Of the Motherland
Faces of the Black Man
Faces of the Black Women

The faces of Ethiopia
And even Nigeria
Sweet faces in Atlanta
Pretty faces in Tanzania

Many beautiful smiles
Many beautiful shades
I'm really talking about
The faces of Black babes

Don't forget my Jamaica
Tobago and Trinidad
And there are a few more
That I must add

Beautiful Black faces
In the Republic of Fuji
Beautiful black faces
In Papua, New Guinea

Beautiful African faces
Around San Francisco Bay
A beautiful face flying next to me
Flying to LA.

Get Through

I tried to call
You are not here
If your were here
This is what
I would say dear

I love talking to you
Longing for us to be near
In love
But distance I fear

What I really want
Is to bring you near
My beautiful dear
Can you hear?

Tried to call
But I couldn't get through,
This is what I would.

Great God

Great God lives
Up in the sky
But our God
Is also close by

So Great God
So far up in the sky
Bless my people
Help us be free, presently

Give us a destiny free
Free of the discrimination
Past and present
Free of slavery and brutality
Past and present

Jesus was
God's earthly son
And through Jesus
Our grace will come

And when our freedom comes
We'll all see
The world is one

Let our freedom come
Oh Great One
Great God, my master and friend
Come save this world from racial sin.

Inspiration for Liberation

Inspiration
Take us to liberation
Take us from stagnation
To a better situation

Inspiration
Take us to liberation
From self destruction
Oppressed Black Nation

Redeem us from
Beating each other down
Inspiration
The way must be found

Divine Inspiration
Cleanse our mind
It's our common sense
We must find

In these days
Help us change our ways
We are in a blind daze
Liberate us from this phase

Inspiration
Move us to liberation
We got it within us
Unite African-American Nation.

Rise Up Mighty People

Rise up mighty people
Rise up from slavery
In our memory
And our history

Rise up mighty people
We have arrived
In a new century
Rise up from gang
And tribal war
Rise up, proud of
Who we are
Grab some education
Take your liberation
In this year, 2002
Let us push on through
Through the gates of freedom
Rise up mighty people.

There is Poetry

There is poetry in me
expressed in my poetry
Like a congress declared attack
on the Republic of Iraq

While here, no homes
for the homeless
and no democracy in Florida
What does America profee or assess?

Why not a regime change
When Blacks were attacked
in the American south
or in per-liberation South Africa

Constructive engagement
Supporting the rand
instead of supporting
the Black Man
When apartheid meant genocide
to a South African Black Man and Woman

Why not a regime change
in the blood filled streets
of an Israeli occupied Palestine
How about regime changing
removal of the occupation

There is a choice
you make peace or war
or do nothing thereby you choose war
Would America attack Israel to free Palestine?

Why not a regime change
right here with fair elections
A diversity celebration
and reparation for the African American nation.

Liberation Blues

Remember that old Plantation
We were dreaming of liberation
It's the promise of our generation
It's political education

From plantation blues
To Black Liberation news
From plantations news
To Black Liberation Blues

They got us in a cell
They got our mind in jail
They sending us to hell
They say there is no bail

From plantation news
To Black Liberation Blues
Pain is Life
In a Black Person's shoes.

Oakland in 2002

Do we know
What to do
About the survival
Of me and you

It is not yet
October of 2002
We have killed 84
How many more

I'm talking about
Oakland
This year's capital
Of brotherly murder
Of the African-American
Black Man

Tell the world
Every Black Man
Woman boy and girl

Stop the fratricide
Stop the homicide
Or how long
Will we survive?

In Frisco
And Richmond too
In Oakland
All over the world too

We have to
Stop the murder
Buy us by me
and you

84 Husbands gone
Cannot call life home
84 Mother's crying
84 families dying

Killing the
Brothers
And the Sisters too

Do you think
About the
Impact
What you do

Murderers
do not go above
Brothers
Where is the love and reparations?

There is Poetry

There is poetry in me
expressed in my poetry
Like a congress declared attack
on the Republic of Iraq

While here, no homes
for the homeless
and no democracy in Florida
What does America profess or assess?

Why not a regime change
When Blacks were attacked
in the American south
or in per-liberation South Africa

Constructive engagement
Supporting the rand
instead of supporting
the Black Man

When apartheid meant genocide
to a South African Black Man and Woman

Why not a regime change
in the blood filled streets
of an Israeli occupied Palestine
How about regime changing
removal of the occupation

There is a choice
to make peace or war
or do nothing thereby you choose war
Would America attack Israel to free Palestine?

Why not a regime change
right here with fair elections
A diversity celebration
and reparations for the African- American nation.

There is Poetry: Part 2

There is a poem
up in me
Expressed
in my poetry

Like unilateralism
white folks go it alone
will poor Black soldiers
die attacking Blacks in Iraq

Will the poor man die?
to make an oil man rich?
what a cost
in human life
In another unjust war
To control the oil for the American car

We remember the pole tax
and Anti Black white attacks
we remember slavery
and still we experience police brutality
and racial discrimination
stereotyping, racial profiling
and the Sheriff's road block
near a Florida polling station
is this really liberation?

There is poetry up
in me expressed
in my poetry.

Why Discriminate?

Why discriminate
When you can educate
And let others
Participate

Why discriminate
When you know
It's a great step
You must take?

Why oppress
And discriminate
When you
could evaluate?

Why hate and
Discriminate
Be for real
Don't be a fake.

Why discriminate
Why not educate
And take the steps
You must take?

Whence We Came

Together we are hundreds
Of millions strong
If we are divided
Discrimination, colonialism and slavery go on

United we are hundreds
Of millions strong
Separated we may not
last too long

African-Americans
From whence we came?
Africa is the root
Of our name

From whence we came
African is our name
Be proud!! No shame
Africa is our roots and fame

I heard a brother say
I no be African
I heard a sister say
I am not African

Black brothers and sisters
All over the world
One people, every man
Woman, boy and girl.

My People What Do You Say

Hey brothers
What do you say?
About the things
That goes on today

Hey sisters
What do you say?
About the things
That happens today

1/3 of the brothers
Too many of the sisters
Victims of the torts
In jail or under the courts

Hey my people
What do you say?
Get it for yourself
Don't worry about no on else?

Until the time
You have to pay
I don't care about them
Is that all you have to say

What about a helping hand
Help your community
Understand
Black woman/Black Man

Hey my people
What do you say?
About what is
Going on today

Hey my people
What do you say?
Improve ourselves
Unite today?
Hey my people, what do you say?

The Beauty of a Sister

When you see her walking
WHEN YOU SEE HER TALKING
Let me tell you mister
That's the beauty of a sister

Think about her wit
Check out her mind
What you will find
Our sister is one of a kind

Like a hurricane
Stronger than a twister
Strength and integrity
Is in the beauty of a sister

Walking with us through history
Sharing with us our destiny
Like a sun, no the moon
She is covered in mystery

So many shades of beauty
To our race, a sense of duty
In so many shapes
A sister's beauty escapes
And that is a shade
That never ever fades

Let me tell you mister
She's stronger than a twister
Stand up! If you agree with me
On the beauty of a sister

Please do not bleach her
Please do not mistreat her
Talking to you my brother
About the beauty of a sister

She's rough dainty and sweet
She's balanced on her feet
I'm not talking about a twister
But the beauty of a sister!

Don't Sing the Blues for Me

Don't sing the blues for me
Don't sing the blues for me
I can sing the blues for myself
I have paid some dues
And I have suffered the blues

Don't sing a sad song for me
I can sing one of my own
Falsely charged for a crime
It happens all the time

Don't write a sad poem for me
I can write my sad song
With a dagger in my back
I'll continue on

I was sold by my friend
I found out in the end
It was a terrible blow
And I was the last to know.

I Don't Like All I See

I don't like all I see
Do you agree with me?
Brother treats Brother like an enemy
I don't like all I see

Like inmates suffering in the cell
Some people feel life is hell
Like sweating in the hot sun
Or living on the run

Like carrying a heavy load
Traveling down a rough road
And those who desire to be free
I don't like all I see

Too much poverty
Too much misery
Too much brutality
I don't like all I see.

Let My People Go

Slave master
Think faster
One thing is for sure
Let My People

Go Slave driver
With your evil soul
Old funky jimmy crow
Let My People Go

Invincible chains
And white man's names
Must this land
Be consumed by flames

Until the time you know
We won't take it any more
All we're asking Jim Crow
Let my people go

Let go of the Africans
Free all the Haitians
Free all the slaves
In unmarked graves

Free the African personality
Free you and me
Slave master no more
Let My People Go.

Their Rhythms? Our Rhythms

Their rhythms
Are our rhythms?
Our rhythms
Are their rhythms?

United African people
All over the world
Rhythms of every Black
Man, women, boy and girl

Rhythms of Africa
Flow through my soul
Rhythms of Africa
Let the world behold

Drum beat rhythms
Of a self loving people
Drumbeats and rhythms
Our survival down through the years

Our struggles for freedom
From Black and White oppressors
Our durability, accountability
Our strategy, destiny and equality

Bouncing like the drums
To the sounds of our inner soul
We are more precious
Than the entire world's gold

A Black woman's hug
Can be so sweet
Black unity is
Black victory

Let the rhythm
Keep pumping
In this poem
We're saying something

Unite Black Man
And we are strong
Our destiny is united
Please understand

Let the love
Continue to flow
So our people can
Survive and grow

Unite the rhythms
Of our souls
And we will achieve
Many of our goals.

Tight Jeans

Tight Jeans, tight meat
Tough Jeans look so sweet
Really tight jeans you know what
I mean Designer Jeans with busting seams

Walking down the street
Look so good to those who see
You got two patches on your hips
And pretty pointed tips.

Tight jeans with a pretty Black Face
Moving with rhythm and grace
Tight jeans cuffed at the base
Tight thighs, with no free space

Tight Jeans on Black Queens
Designer jeans with busting seams
Looking so sweet
Tough jeans with busting seams.

Dedicated to Nigerian (Spinsters) young adult women
I saw in Nigeria wearing tight jeans.

Black Liberation or White Supremacy:
Voice Your Choice
Dedicated to Apolitical and Apathetic Black People

What are you really for?
Where do you stand?
Are you on the fence?
Black Woman/Black Man?

Black Liberation
Is it your choice?
Speak with a national
United Voice

White supremacy
Is a white fantasy?
Black Liberation will come with Black Unity

But don't sit on the fence
Cause times are too tense
Things will come to a head
Black Liberation or White Supremacy your dead

The Choice
Is for you to take
The decision
Is yours to make

Unity is the key
For you and me
If we are ever
Going to be free

Black Liberation or
White Supremacy
You can voice your choice
Or continue acting foolishly

It's the choice
Of the eighties
A test of political will
If you're for the real deal.

Black is Black

North or South
East or West
Let's hook up
For peace and progress
Brothers and Sisters
We need to have a chat
Let's hook up cause
Black is Black.

Rough Days for Me

Some days are so dreary
No sun to shine
Some days are so bright
And everything's fine

Some days are so long
They drag on and on
And there are some days
I wish I stayed at home

Some days are so tough
Some days are so rough
Some days are full of misery
And, you know homie

Some days are so gloomy
Some days are so dreary
Some days are so gray
Rough days for me.

Thank God for Melanin

One day before I was 10
I was called darkie
By my classmates
Who make childish mistakes

Vaughn, Clifford and I
Labeled as the darkies
Made to feel ashamed
Of what is our fame

I cried a thousand tears
I asked God why
Why did you color me Black?
Cause if you're Black, they say get back!

And now I am 31
Our battle is yet to be won
Though more work must be done
I am the proud one

Thank God for my Black skin
Thank God for Melanin
Thank God for my Black Skin
Thank God for Melanin.

Liberate Black History

In the
not too distant future
Our descendants will study
the story of our modern misery

How did they survive?
How could they thrive?
They will ask
How did we stay alive

And how did we resist?
Those who persist
In holding our people down
On American ground?

Let's join together
Once more my friend
for a liberated Black history
must be our end.

Re-launch our movement
Attack their government mismanagement
This is no joke
but an open indictment

Liberate Black History
Don't forget the contemporary
dynamics of Black life
Fruit of the oppressed Blackberry.

For when they look back
make sure they see
Our struggle for Black liberation
In a land of disguised white slavery.

Afroan Patriots

African Patriots
Patriots of the Black Nation
Black Patriots
Fighting for Black Liberation

Afroan Patriots
Another brother's been shot
We need to unite a whole lot
A call to Afroan Patriots

Patriots for a white nation
No patriots of the Black Nation
Afroan Patriots
Fighting for Black Nation.

Black History Goes On

Black history goes on
hold on to your tone
Black folks go on
Black history goes on

Black is our history
from Africa our Black star
to America
where we are

Black history moves
walking down third and palou
Black history grooves
Black history is the blues

Black history goes on
In every Black poem
Black History goes on
in every Black song

Black history expands
When Black Folks take control
Black history is old
Black History is the news

Black history is heavy
It's about trying to be free
In a land
of disguised slavery

It's a continuing story
Joining together is Black Glory
Black folks hold on
Black history goes on.

The Spirit of Africa

The spirit of Africa
Lives in our soul
Although some of us
Are misnamed Negro

The spirit arose
From the Niger
Was sold to a plantation
Facing the Mississippi

The Spirit of Africa lives
Picking cotton in them fields
The spirit of Africa lives
When the oppressor kills

The spirit of Africa lives
In our Black beautiful skin
In the Black community
we are all kin

Look at our African rhythm
Look at the resistance we give
Look at our strong soul
Can't die, we have to live

Look at our durability
Though we need more unity
Reach for the freedom we seek
It is our destiny

The spirit of Africa
Inside our tortured soul
Inside our brainwashed mind
Since the beginning of time

The spirit lives
Inside of you and me
The spirit gives us
one destiny

The spirit lives
We have African blood
Rushing like a river
In every child we deliver.

The Spirit of Africa

The spirit lives
in the blood we shed.
The spirit of Africa lives
In the hair on our head.

My Beautiful Wife

I want to
See eye to eye
With you
I want to see
What you see
I want you
To see what I see

Eye to eye
Nose to nose
Lips to lips
Love to love

I want to see
You yesterday
Today
And tomorrow

Like a bright sunny day
I want you to
Come my way

My African queen
Brand new thing
My beautiful new wife
For the rest of my life.

Written 10/24/03 10:30pm

Nothing

Nothing beats a failure
But a real good try
That is the truth
You cannot deny

There are many ways
To skin a cat
Many many ways
To destroy a rat

From Miami to Memphis
White feet in Black teeth
Racist intimidation
A hell of a situation

8:00am report to your station
Ignore your ugly situation
Are you really free in this nation
Where is the route to Liberation

Nothing beats a failure
But a real good try
We have a choice to live or die
To live or die

Don't ignore our people's cry
My people are very dry
The day of Black sanity
Is the day we try Black Unity.

I am A Dissident

About racist white supremacy
The hypocrisy of the US democracy
If you are the president
I AM A DISSIDENT

Justice in society
Peace through equality
End police brutality
Give us liberty!!!!!

You see Black people in oppression
Where is the white concession?
If you are the President
I AM A DISSIDENT.

This poem was written in the Reagan years.

Walk Together My People

Walk together my people
In a lion's den
Until we get liberation
Don't make a lion your friend

Walk together my people
Work together for success
Walk together my people
Let us try our very best

Walk together my people
In a dangerous battle zone
Walk together my people
We can make it on our own

Walk together my people
We are our only friends
Talk together my people
we can solve our problems

Stick together my people
In a land of police brutality
Struggle together my people
One day we will be free

Walk together my people
In an evil and violent land
Walk together my people
In the land of uncle Sam

Stay together Black People
Let no one tell you it's a sin
Don't make a lion your friend
While we live in a lion's den.

I Know You Know Why

Sweet as a pretty flower
Something sweet has gone sour
There is no need to cry
When it ends we say bye bye

One tear may fall, from her eye
There is no need to cry
So many relationships die
I know you know why

You got to do your thing
What we had was only a fling
There is no pain only a sting
You are free to do your thing

I know you know why
I said good-bye

Son of Africa

Bob Marley of Jamaica
Dedicated to the memory of Bob Marley

Bob Marley
Son of Africa
Black Man for Freedom
Fighting for our rights
In Babylon the white man's kingdom
His weapon was reason
he was against racial treason
He fought the oppressors
He defeated aggressors
Acknowledging freedom's call
Bob Marley standing tall
In his life's time
Fighting for our kind
Bob Marley
Son of Africa
Bob Marley
Son of Jamaica
He put his foot down in Africa
He put his foot down in England
When his time was near him
Bob Marley remembered Harlem
With poems of Black Freedom
for all people in the white man's kingdom
For all Blacks in the west
who are the most oppressed

And all African People
cause this system is unequal
Defying the powers that be
Asserting our right to be free
Hearing Africa's call
Bob Marley Stands Tall.

Oppressive Regimes

African Haitians sailing
running away from a young tyrant
Look at Reagan turning them back
A tyrant supported by the U.S. President

And Black South Africans
Bombing the Boer Republic
The brothers keep on bombing
The boers cannot stop it

Black people's blood
On their repressive hands
Repressive governments
On peaceful lands

Bowevils and the President
Conspire and connive
To hang Black People
In broad daylight

Calling on progressive Blacks
Check out the scene
Calling for the overthrow
Of undemocratic regimes

If and when it is possible
Use political means
Calling for the over throw
Of all oppressive regimes.

Waiting for You

I'm a do
What I want
To do and that is
wait on you

You got a
Lot to go through
You are
So far away too

And as soon
As you come in
You'll make my life
An earthly heaven

I am going to
Wait on you
I feel what
You're going through

I want to
See you and hold you too
So I'm waiting
For you.

Dedicated to Ese Ohe Grace Mamodu

History to Destiny Through Afrocentric Poetry

This collection of poetry by Larry Ukali Johnson-Redd spans a thirty-year process of reflection and critique on the condition of Black folks in the U.S. and around the world, centered in a progressive African philosophical context that balance politics, emotions and sensuality.

Amen-Ra Theological Seminary Press
10920 Wilshire Boulevard, Suite 150-9132
Los Angeles, California 90024-6502

www.ingramcontent.com/pod-product-compliance
Lightning Source LLC
Chambersburg PA
CBHW051133120626
46547CB00012B/782